D0896823

Door to Door

Door to Door

a novel by Tobi Tobin

POCKET BOOKS

New York · London · Toronto · Sydney · Singapore

For Henry,

The most beautiful man I have ever known.
The love of my life, my muse, my friend, my lover.
Loving you has been the best decision I ever made . . .

ACKNOWLEDGMENTS

As I write these acknowledgments, I feel so blessed and grateful to have all of you in my life. Your friendship and support has meant so much to me. Without it, writing this novel would not have been possible. To Fawn, thank you for your constant encouragement and friendship. I will always love you. Your smile, your laughter and hugs will stay with me forever. You have been a great gift to me. To Jacob, because of you this book was published. Thank you for making me a better writer and for being the best editor any writer could hope for. Your help, support, and friendship I will never forget. To Rhea, what a long journey it's been. You sold this book, you made it happen, you're a star. I'll always love you. Thank you. To my mom, no words can be said for how grateful I am to you for always believing in the book and me. I love you. To Karan, what would I do without you? How could I get through a day without your support and friendship? You mean so much to me. You're so beautiful. To Marni, you're the best. I adore you. Thank you for every phone call, all your advice, encouragement and help. To Helena, how do I thank you. There are no words. I love you so much, my mentor, my friend, without you this would not have been possible. Nothing will ever separate us. To Noelle, thank you for all your support and friendship. Tell it like it is, girl, it keeps me alive. To Susan, your prayers and friendship made this possible. I love you. To Janusz, thank you for every new day that you showed me. For every smile that we shared together and for the few times I dared to breathe. You'll always be in my heart. To Hank, thank you, thank you, thank you for making me laugh, for trusting me, loving me and being such a good friend. To Meghan and Spoonie, I love you both so much. Thank you for every moment that I've shared with you. To Gweniver, the most important moment of my life I shared with you. Without you, this book would not have been possible. Thank you for your support and prayers. To Vivian, thank you for all your years of friendship and support. I cherish you. To Kate, you're the best. You're beautiful, sweet, kind and lovely. Thank you for always being there for me. To Irmelin, thank you for your friendship and long walks on the beach. I love you. To Beth and Tag, for the many years of support, friendship, laughs, cries, kindness and the many years we will share together yet to come. To Lisa, for the many farm stories, crazy phone calls, friendship, support, kindness, beautiful days, truthfulness, good food, and helping all my dreams come true. I love you. To Kerry, for everlasting friendship, truth, kindness, support, encouragement, thoughtfulness and always being there for me. I love and adore you. Thank you. To Jonathan and Vic and all my friends at Malibu Kitchen on Sunday mornings. Thank you for your support. To all my friends that knew me when: I love you.

EXT. A BAR, LOS ANGELES, CA

VOICE-OVER

The end is in every great beginning. I think
you must carry the ending with you to start.
But, in this particular case, the end was
slowly creeping closer, each day, each night,
each hour. I now believe there is a weight
you must carry in any journey that is worth-
while. However, there is also a peace in
knowing there will be an ending. When does
it end? It ends when you say so.

I ran the Door. . . . I ran the Door for six
grueling years of my life. The story is hard
to tell because it has no center, it has no
hope, it's just a story suspended in air. But it
was that air that was different. The smoke
that lingered in the darkness of a closing
bar, the spilt beer, the dirty ashtrays, and the
leftover food in bus pans waiting for a rinse.
That was the air. The air apparent.

* * *

The loud music goes off, you're done for the night, cold, sad, tired. You stare, you stare at nothing, you feel nothing. None of the guys talk to you, they know not to. You're head of the Door. You just finished talking to over a thousand people in six hours. You count the cash, you hand out the envelopes, collect the walkies, stash the clickers, pull in the ropes, clear out the staff, gather the bulletproof vests, pull out the clips, lock up the metal, wait for security to have the last drink, and walk out. You do it over and over again every time the music shuts off and the bar clears out. But I did it because I was a survivor, and I would never have stopped doing it if I hadn't discovered what that really meant. This is my story, this is my riff, this was me, and still some days is . . .

BASIC RULES
(relating to, or forming the base or essence)

I had some basic rules at the Door, things that never changed: Two guys outside with me, I pick 'em, and they are there for a reason. Smart first, fast, good eye, they're my back eyes when I talk. They watch me, then the crowd. They don't speak, ever, unless I say so; they don't touch the ropes—unless I say so; and most importantly, they better fuckin' watch the crowd. When I did my first Door, I had two guys with me outside and four inside. Head of security stayed inside, on walkie-talkie with me. If they were good, they lasted. And if they were just in it for a job, they quit like a bunch of pussies. Usually they were there for a reason. I hated the inside, I guess that's why I ran a Door. But some of the guys were just inside. I never understood those guys, and why they liked it so much, fuckin' smoke everywhere, loud music vibrating in your ear; shit, most of the guys ended up with hearing problems. It wasn't until the '90s that they started wearing earplugs, and even then those never lasted.

Anyway, outside was no thrill either. You had to deal with the weather, cold, fuckin' cold, and windy. No matter what time of year it was, it was always bad for the clubs. The best Doors were street Doors, as they looked the best, but for a Door person, they sucked. No protection. Every new Door I did I always checked out the street it was on, the building it was next to and the alleyways surrounding it, 'cause it mattered. I looked for plants out front of the Door, I asked for black mats on the cement to keep our feet warm, and I checked out the pavement to see if it was flat or on an angle, 'cause if it was on an angle your back would hurt all night long. There were so many factors that went into a given Door. For example, the club owners might love bushes at the Door, but they were the worst fuckin' nightmare because you couldn't see around them or behind them, which left leeway for trouble. You live in constant fear. Who did you piss off the night before? Who wants to kill you? Or your constant list of people who hate you because no matter what, at some point they pissed you off, and they are never getting in—never. And if you work as long as I did, that could put a real cramp in your social life if I didn't think fondly of you or your little group. However, from time to time there were some repercussions for my behavior which I really didn't care for, but at least I knew which asshole could cause such a cramp in my evening. See, when some rat fink little prick got bent out of shape for not getting in he might get the cute idea to call the fire department and have a little chat with them regarding the capacity of my club, and better yet, the amount of people standing out on the street. The complaint would go something like this: "Hello, my name is loser. Why? Well, because I stand on a street corner on a Friday night in Los Angeles with nothing better to do than to call the local fire department to complain about the nightclub across the street with what looks to be a potential fire hazard inside. I know this information because being the loser I am and never being allowed into one of these establishments, I make these calls frequently and am accustomed to ratting out Door persons who disgrace me in front of my friends and my hideous ego, which I am trying to improve by actually getting picked out of a crowd to enter one of these places. So here's the address. This is just a concerned citizen calling to inform the fire department of this potentially dangerous situation. Thank you. Have a nice night."

> FIRE MARSHALL
> What kind of numbers do we have in here tonight? Mind if I take a look around and check the clickers?

> TOBI
> Not at all, my friend, come on in and take the tour.

> FIRE MARSHALL
> What's the capacity here?

> TOBI
> Ninety-eight.

> FIRE MARSHALL
> Get some people out of here or we'll shut you down. Get them out of here now.

> TOBI
> Yes, sir.

> FIRE MARSHALL
> Let's have a little chat. Meet me in the alley.

> TOBI
> Who called?

                    FIRE MARSHALL
Some guy.

                         TOBI
What time?

                    FIRE MARSHALL
9:40.

                         TOBI
From what phone?

                    FIRE MARSHALL
Across the street.

                         TOBI
Thanks!

                    FIRE MARSHALL
Any time. Keep the club clean and the
numbers down. What'a ya got for me?

                         TOBI
Nothing.

                    FIRE MARSHALL
Okay, see ya.

                         TOBI
See ya.

* * *

They weren't supposed to tell you who called, but of course they did. Why? Payback. Everybody was shaking everybody else's hand. If I gave them information on drug dealers, prostitutes, vagrants or drive-bys, they left my clubs alone.

I was the thinker, the one who had to make it work; the guys, they could have fun, check out the girls, talk about the night before, shoot the shit, tell jokes. I had to keep it straight. But when the shit hit the fan, it was the guys that had to fight. I liked fighters, but fighters who didn't fight. There's a difference. See, if I knew that one of the guys was high strung, they weren't at the Front Door. That would mean Inside. At the Front Door, you've got to have guys that are tough as shit and can protect you but also play by the rules. They gotta look good too. New York style, classy, modern-day gangster shit, 'cause that's what we thought we were. We had to think something, we stood all night long talking about our lives, our dreams, where we grew up, where we were going, and how we were getting there. Each one of us had a story and it usually changed nightly, but the longer we worked together and the longer we dreamed together, the faster we thought we were getting out. We wanted out of our past, out of our own way, and especially out of doing the Door, and the more we talked about it the better it made us feel. We justified it. We justified what we were doing by thinking it was only temporary, just holding on until our personal dreams became a reality. Just doing what we were told. Even knowing it was wrong, we still found a different reason each and every night to speak the hideous words we needed to speak so we could do it again for another eight hours, until we could once again forget the crime we were committing by choosing people by their race, jobs, wardrobe, beauty, fame and anything else that had nothing to do with humanity but everything to do with getting in the Door.

BILLY

It's gonna be a cold one tonight, kids,
Boston chilly.

DANIEL

Speaking of Boston, you Irish fuck, did you
get the score?

BILLY

I got the score for you, you guinea pig, and
it's right here between my legs, all eight
inches of it!

Daniel grabs his crotch.

DANIEL

Quit fuckin' around, what's the score? Did
you tell Jonnie to put the game on?

BILLY

Yeah, I told him, but he says the boss wants
MTV or some shit like that, he said he'd
check the scores later and let us know.

DANIEL

Ah, fuck him, fuck 'em all, shit it's cold
already.
    (Daniel makes a fist and slaps his black
    leather gloves together.)
That's right, sissy, so I hope your mother
dressed you warm for school.

BILLY

So what's up with you, Tobs, gotten laid
lately?

TOBI

Now how the fuck am I supposed to get
laid with you assholes around me all the
time, you think some guy is just not gonna
notice that I have fifteen security guys pro-
tecting me at all times? Yeah, that'll
happen . . .

DANIEL

So you're not getting laid, then what else is
up, sister?

TOBI

Same old shit, not enough money to make
it work for me, can't find a way out of this
fuckin' hell, and I'm tired.

DANIEL

Tobs, you're not tired, you're burnt, sister,
you're just burnt!
(Daniel gives Tobi a hug.)
You know what you need, sweet pea? A
vodka. Billy, run in and get Tobs her vodka,
and tell that fuck Jonnie to give you the
score.

Billy goes inside.

TOBI

(Staring at a streetlight)

You know what it is, Daniel? I can't smell
Michigan anymore. I can't smell it, I can't
feel it, I can't remember what it tastes like,
and worse, I don't really know if I care.
You know I spend hours talking to Will,
that homeless guy you both see me shooting
the shit with, and you know what? I'm the
one who's homeless, I'm the one who's lost;
Will's not lost, his home is where he makes
it day after day. My home slips away more
and more every moment that I spend here
at the Door trying to remember it. Trying to
remember the way my grandpa's Virginia
ham smelled on Sunday mornings on the
ranch or the way my grandmother looked
sitting in the old glider, you know, the kind
from the fifties with those plastic plaid belts
that run in between the metal parts. Those
are the things I miss, that's who I am, a
fuckin' summer raspberry-pickin' girl, you
know, and I can't find that in me today, and
I can't see that on me today. I just feel this

(points to her long black winter overcoat,
black leather men's gloves, and raises her
clipboard.)

I mean this is now, this is what I choose,
but it's just not who I am.

DANIEL

I'll tell you, Tobs, that's one sad fuckin'

little tale you're spooling out over there.
Save some tears for me, will ya!

TOBI

Hey, Daniel, I heard you hate being Inside,
'cause you know, I was thinkin' that maybe
you'd like to switch your tight ass with ol'
Gater Inside, 'cause from what I hear, he's
dying to be out here with poor little ol' me.
What do you think about that, little girl?

DANIEL

I think you'd miss me.

Tobi takes a swing at Daniel.

TOBI

I think you're right, you little fuck, so I
guess you'll just have to listen to my sob
stories all fuckin' night long and like it.
Where's Billy? He's always fuckin' around.
Call him in on line two, it's getting busy
and I want that vodka.

I had a good eye for security guys. I got lucky with most of the
guys I ever worked with. They were the best Front Door guys
too. Front Door guys usually started Inside. Lots of long nights
Inside, lots of clubs under their belts before they were outside at
the Front Door. None of them, however, had worked with a
woman. And for the most part that meant more fights for them.
Covering the back for one of your other guys was one thing, but
defending a woman was another. So, the first night they watched
me, listened to me, stood beside me, opened the ropes for me,

stepped in front for me, and the second night they believed in me. Why? It was the opposite, I kept them out of fights. Talking, negotiating, and making deals all night long. But sometimes we had to fight, and we knew when and how, and when that happened I would have hated being on the other end. Not only were they defending a woman, they stuck together like glue. Years and years of being on the same team, and many long nights of taking shit from drunk assholes. When we fought, we all fought. Inside came out, Outside went in, wherever the action was. It usually got pretty messy too, until the cops arrived. They never did anything, though. They were on our side. Shit, we were doing them a favor. "One less drunk on the streets for the night" was their attitude. We all felt like shit after a night with a fight. That was a hard night. Usually, someone got hurt, bit, hit, or scratched. All of it sucked. And for what? Well, that's what hit us at the end of the night. It wasn't so much the fight, it was what we were fighting for. None of us really knew. . . .

I usually got to the club an hour early, sat at the bar and stared. A quiet stare at nothing. I loved the club then, all clean, the lights low, and the bartenders setting up the bar, cleaning glasses, filling the top-shelf bottles of liquor with the cheap call-brand booze and counting their banks. I'd pick a place at the bar, usually next to my favorite bartender, and order a Coke. I knew it was going to be a long night and I needed something to stay up, and cocaine wasn't my thing. I drank, but it was never a problem. Sometimes I ate, but usually I ate early, around four o'clock; that way I could think clearly and not get tired. I picked up the clipboard, the guest list, my walkie-talkie, and my clickers. My gear, that was it, that's what I depended on for six years. What I didn't know at the time was how much those things would mean to me. Each one of those things was saturated with meaning. The clipboard, that was the big one, it said head of the Door. You looked at it a thousand times a night, and it could save your ass all night long. Lies, that's what the clipboard was all about, lies. A chance to think, check the list, pause, time to think of the lie, weigh the lie, think of a line, move on, next, look up, say the lie, move on, next. Check the list, check the list all fuckin' night long. But it was a lie. I never needed to check the list. I would memorize the list before I started. I was dyslexic but developed a nearly photographic memory. The list was time, precious time, and the crowd thought it was the answer. But it was never the answer, it was the lie. It was all in the lie. It was how you told the lie, how your body moved when you delivered the lie, how your hands gestured during the lie, and the most important part of the lie, the stare. You had to stare right into their eyes and lie, never letting your eyes waver until the lie had been accepted. Move on and lie to the next person standing behind them to confirm the first lie, pause, believe the lie, and let them believe the lie.

It wasn't just lying I was good at either. It was my body language too, my hands, my tone of voice, the way I'd get close to you. It happened fast. I made decisions on other people coming to the Door while I was still talking to someone else. That was the show, the rap. I talked, I moved. I watched cars on the street, I looked at the list, I joked with the guys, I had the count from the Door in my head. On and on, all night long, repeating the same lines to different faces, fixing, adjusting my lie, timing the lie, perfecting the lie.

I got the dinner reservations in, I got kisses, handshakes, hellos, hugs, introductions, add-ons, watch-out-fors, have-you-seens, by-the-ways, again and again, as I opened the Door. That was early, though. Every hour had its activity. Eight o'clock you came in, set up, got your guest list for the night. I liked mine short, under twenty names. Names I knew, though I liked surprises. If I knew someone good was coming in, like a famous actor or rock star, it would change the whole night, I'd change the Door. Depending on who it was, maybe I'd save space, add more girls, less guys, save time, push back. Different situations required different tactics. For a Door person, it was all about space. Numbers, crowd, the ratio of men to women, the mix. Every time I said yes or no, I had to have a reason. That's what made a club and the Door. I'd highlight names, cross out names, make notes next to the names: producer, PG (pretty girl), dir (director), AH (asshole), M (model), A (actor), AA (access agent), lay (lawyer), rock (rock star), bb (basketball), foot (football), hoc (hockey), writer, plus how many, and any special notes like what time they were coming in and who with and what kind of car they drove and which Door you were going to bring them in, which table they were going to sit at, and so forth. Then I'd usually check in with the owners and ask about any personal friends or people not on the list, and that was it. Time to relax, sit at the bar, stop talking, stare, order a drink, nod and think. I used to nod a lot, I just knew what you were going to say before you would say it. So any talk about the night before, I hated it. It was over, on to the next. . . . I had to live that way. I never looked back. I wanted to be left alone in the club before the night began, just a few words to the bartenders, that was it. I needed the time to feel my own silence. To see the bar quiet and still. I needed to imagine the club at all hours of the night, from beginning to end, all counts of clickers, all counts of chairs, and open exits available to me for emergencies. Security checked in fifteen minutes before we headed outside; we checked the walkie-talkies, checked the club, opened the exits, checked the back Door, talked to the kitchen, greeted the hostess, the waiters, the bartenders, got coffee, put our gloves on, put our coats on, moved the stands out, put the ropes up, shut the door, called in security check, set the clickers, set the fake clickers, waited. . . .

TOBI

Listen up, you guys, I wanna see shit
tonight that's coming at me from a mile
away. I wanna see cars on the street before
they're in valet. I wanna see groups of girls
from a block away. I wanna see cash close
to me, so pay attention, 'cause I'm working
it tonight, boys, and I don't want any fuckups. I got the boss all over my ass about
too many men in the club and you know
what that is, my little princess, because
both you fucks are telling all your fuckin'
little girly ass friends to come down and see
your white ass standing at the Door, and
I'm telling you, that's it. Show's over, girls,
because we're getting too many guys in too
early and it's fuckin' me up, so if you want
your friends in tell them to come on a
Wednesday night, not Thursday, 'cause I
can't do it. (Looks down at the list.) Oh
fuck, could this list be longer tonight. I hate
this time of night, I hate the waiting, I hate
this hour before nine, it's like being the lion
behind the gate waiting for the steak. Why
don't some of these fucks come a little earlier than nine, you know I feel like telling
them the key to getting in any club is to
come early, but you know if I did tell them
that, they'd still come at nine. I'm totally
PMS. (Looking down the street.) Oh fuck,
here comes that shithead from last night,
when is this guy gonna get it, huh? I'm not

letting that fuck in, and don't you guys
touch those ropes . . .

MAN

Hey, what's up? Yeah, I'm on the list, I'm
having dinner here.

TOBI

What's the name?

MAN

Simms, Gregory Simms, I'm meeting my
agent here for dinner.

TOBI

(checking the list, then looking directly in
his eyes)
Simms, I don't see a Simms on the list.

MAN

Well, look, I'm meeting my agent here and
we're having dinner here at eight.

TOBI

Sorry, I don't have a Simms on the list, can
you excuse me a minute?
(speaking with another person approaching
the Door)
What's the name? Brill, what time? Eight-
thirty? Come right in, Mr. Brill.

TOBI
(back to Simms)
So look, like I told you, you're not on the
list.

SIMMS
You just let that guy in.

TOBI
He's on the list.

SIMMS
But so am I, I'm supposed to be on the list.

TOBI
Sorry, your name's not here.

SIMMS
I want to speak with the manager.

TOBI
I'm the manager. And as far as I can see,
we've already spoken.

SIMMS
Look, what's it gonna take to get in here so
that I can meet my agent and have dinner?

TOBI
I told you, your name's not on my list.

SIMMS
(getting agitated)
But my name is on the list.

TOBI
Sorry, your name's not on the list.

SIMMS
Fuck it, and fuck this club, and fuck you too.

TOBI
Any time, buddy, I could use a good
fuck . . .

BILLY
That fuck just doesn't get it, does he?

TOBI
Yeah, he gets it, but he doesn't want to accept
it. But that's the last you'll see of him, they
never come back after they finally get it, but
some go down harder than others, my friend.

BILLY
Why don't you like that guy?

TOBI
'Cause he's desperate, and you never let
desperate Inside. Never let them see you
sweat, man, just like the commercial says.
Never let anyone see you sweat . . . it's a
sign of weakness.

BILLY
Not always, man, not always.

TOBI
Yeah, well, you try tearing Desperate off
some naive starlet just looking for a fun
night out with the girls and she's gotta run
into that desperate fuck trying to talk her
up at the bar, feeding her one line of bullshit after the next, and you tell me what's
easier, to not let him in or kick his ass out.
Let me tell you, darling, the answer is not
to let the fucker in . . .

BILLY
Right again, sister, you go, girl!

TOBI
Kiss my sweet ass. Listen, if someone brings
candy tonight at the Door, let them in, I'm
dying for a piece of chocolate.

DANIEL
So all it takes is chocolate to get in?

TOBI
(smiling)
Sometimes!

The night started off like an explosion. First you got set, the ritual, every night over and over. The way you'd do things, the way
you'd come in, what you wore, what guys were on, what night it

was, what day of the week it was, that was big, 'cause it mattered. Wednesday through Saturday, there was a difference in the crowd. Well, it is if you set it up that way, and I did. See, you set the game, you decide what the room looks like, 'cause it's your ass in the end anyway, so why not make it great, and the fact is, they liked it that way (the crowd). They just liked being told where to go and how to get there. That's all, just a little help along the way. It's amazing to me the thoughts I had at the Door. It's funny and sad to think all at the same time I smiled that big fuckin' Kansas smile at them night after night, welcoming them into the pit of hell, and inside I was dying. Yeah, there were rules, when I could pack the club, et cetera. Usually, after eleven o'clock, I'd trash the place. That meant all your good reservations were in and it was time to start the second show. They were so different—the A team and the B team— shit, some nights there was even a C team. But whatever team you were on, at least you got it, and for the most part, you never knew you were even on a team anyway, only I did. I was the fucking captain and I picked the teams accordingly. Only the A team sort of picked itself. You see, the A team had lots of requirements, but mostly power-based, and what kind of power you had in Hollywood determined your worth to me and my club.

So what were the requirements? For men, they had to have style, lots of style of their own. I determined this by the clothes they wore, the cars they drove, the job they had, and the girls they brought with them, and if they knew my real name or they used the fake one. Most people used my fake Door name (Susan); however, the A team knew my name and used it, and a select few actors, directors, producers, and a couple of writers had my cell phone number at the Door. The A team consisted mostly of actors, directors, producers, athletes, musicians, lawyers, famous people in general, and some regulars. This was the most important part of the club, because without them there was no club, and with just a few of them in the club you were set for the night. The women on the A team were equally as important as the men, but in a completely different way. Beauty was their power, and heavily connected didn't hurt either. Girlfriend of so-and-so, daughter of this director or that producer, wife of that movie star, girl that's having an affair with that guy that always comes in, ex-wife of that actor, girl that lives with that producer, that girl that brings in actors all the time, those girls that hang out with Jack Nicholson all the time, the bunnies, the models, the actresses, the hookers, the dancers, and just the pretty fluff that could fill my clubs for a few hours and sell drinks, that was money. Women equal money in any club anywhere in the world, because without them, men don't stay and they don't pay, so they say! So, that was their job and the A team was complete. I always thought there was a reason, too, why these people were considered A list, and for the most part you'd think they would be the worst, but it was the opposite really, it was the rest of the crowd that made me sick. Still, I loved it all. That was the gig, you hated it, but you were in, like selling your soul to the devil. One day you wake up and you're in it, and you like it, you live it, you believe it, and then slowly you sell, and you sell, and you sell, and then what's left? It doesn't matter, because one great night with the A team in, your club is packed with all the right people, the owners are happy, and you're a fuckin' star.

But I ran my clubs straight up, no bullshit. I knew it was a team effort, me and the guys, and everyone had to pull their weight; not the owners, however, they thought they were with us, but they weren't. Oh sure, we'd protect them from the sleazebags that gave them money for getting the joint together, or the ex-girlfriends or the landlords or the city officials, but they didn't stop the bullet, we did, if you know what I mean. So a good night had a lot to offer.

COUNTRY CLUBS AND HAND-ME-DOWNS

When I close my eyes and remember Bloomfield Hills, Michigan, I see first the dirt road that leads to the house I was raised in. I see the large evergreens that line the street and smell the oil freshly laid by city trucks. I hear loud beeping noises signaling their presence on our street. Then I see myself running down the long driveway to the big steel mailbox to collect the mail and pick up the *Detroit Free Press*. I look back at the house and hear my grandmother calling out my name. I am ten years old. I follow the length of the house and I see the freshly painted, white, three-car garage and the circular drive that leads to the front door. I see the side entrance with the Dutch doors and remember the top lock that was always stuck. I see the mail room attached to the garage for packages, I see the cubbyhole behind the black iron stool in which we hid a key, and sometimes ourselves, the large, sprawling lawns with perfectly landscaped gardens. I see the hitching post. A little black man holding a lantern. He wears white riding pants and a red tail coat and a black top hat. He has bright red lips and pearly white teeth and a big smile on his face. I like to tie Twiggy's leash to the iron ring in the little man's hand. I look over the garage and see the bald eagle with his black iron wings outstretched from east to west. I stare at a nest of blue jays. I sit down in the driveway on the hot black pavement in July and look into the sky. I try to look over the rooftop, but the weather vane catches my eye. The rooster is cocking his head back. I hear the sound in my head. I copy the rooster, cocking my head back and making loud cock a doodle dos until I tire. I am confused by the rooster as I stare at him from different angles. I stand up with my arms stretched out to determine which way is north and which is south by the arrows, but I am defeated. I am left again without the answer, not knowing that I'll never be able to see the arrows the same way someone else does, someone without my disability, someone without my dyslexia.

With the ease of my ten-year-old body I rest on the pavement, not feeling a bone ache or the unwanted fat that surrounds me now. I lose sight of the rooster and am free in the heavens with the clouds that grab me and the ocean blue sky on which I paint my dreams. I imagine myself grown: my eighteenth birthday, getting my first car, tying on my prom dress, my hair in pretty pink ribbons like my Barbie, my mother and father together again, happy, waving good-bye as I climb the steps to an Ivy League building. I reach with both hands into the sky to touch the clouds, to capture my dreams and bring them into my chest. The clouds move through me and over me, and though I struggle to grab them my dreams float by and I wonder if I'll ever be able to catch just one of them. My only worry is that the sun will eventually go down and I will once again have to wait twelve hours to paint my dreams in the lucid sky.

GRANDMA

Tobi, Kane, it's time for dinner. (under her breath) Where on God's earth are those children? As if this pheasant can just wait upon them. God knows they sure as heck aren't waiting upon the Lord out there.

(yelling)

Kids, come on in, it's getting dark out there and you're gonna catch your death. You know some children aren't as lucky as you two to be getting all this good food every night. Not everyone is as fortunate as you two kids, just remember that. Now come on in and help me set the table. Your grandfather's gonna be home any minute.

TOBI

Grandma?

GRANDMA

Yes?

TOBI

How come you have so many plastic containers and glass bottles under the sink? I've never seen you use one of those before, ever . . .

GRANDMA

Well, if you two kids had lived through a war, then you might begin to appreciate some things differently. Those glass bottles and containers were hard to come by in those days, so I guess I'll just keep 'em 'cause I still think they're valuable. You'll see, one day the littlest things will mean so much to you, especially if you can't have them anymore.

TOBI
What else was valuable to you then?

GRANDMA
My family, my sisters and brothers, our
home and any food that we could get to
eat, 'cause money wasn't so easy to come
by then, my father couldn't always find
work and it got mighty cold in the winter
sometimes.

KANE
Grandma, what's for dinner?

GRANDMA
Pheasant. Your grandfather went hunting
and brought home a whole bunch of 'em.
So that's what we're having tonight, kiddo,
and some brussels sprouts and red beets
from the garden up north.

TOBI
Grandma, has Mom called?

GRANDMA
Yes, she called earlier and said she'd be
home after dinner and if you kids wanted
you could watch *The Brady Bunch* and *The
Partridge Family* before you go to bed.

KANE
Why is she always coming home so late?

GRANDMA
She's gotta work to help you kids out.
Someone's gotta take care of you two, and
your mother does it all by herself. Now
when you both grow up and have your own
families, you'll know how hard it can be
sometimes.

KANE
But I miss her, and she's always gone.

GRANDMA
Now both of you quit your whining and
hurry up and eat before your food gets cold
and your grandfather gets home and sees
those plates full of food . . .

TOBI
Grandma, can we have grilled cheese sandwiches tomorrow for dinner? I'm sick of
pheasant . . .

GRANDMA
We'll see. But first you're gonna have to
make it into the Clean Plate Club before we
start talkin' grilled cheese sandwiches for
dinner, young lady. And don't forget those
beets, I had to bend down half a dozen
times to pull those out of the ground and
let me tell you, it was hot outside. And
don't tell your grandfather when he walks
in that door that we forgot to say grace, or

that'll be the end of all of us. Now come
on, enough gabbin' and more eatin'.

TOBI
Did my Dad call today?

GRANDMA
No, honey, he didn't, now that's enough,
eat up or you kids can forget the TV.

To be from Bloomfield Hills, Michigan, was a privileged life. At
least that's what you were led to believe from what the adults
said. It's the kind of place that, to this day, if I tell people where
I'm from I'm branded right there on the spot: rich Wasp, well
educated, family likely in the upper ranks of the automotive business. Growing up in this fabulous place of make-believe and trying to get a grasp on the real world was a feat in itself, but at the
same time it was always explained to me that I would never need
to leave this utopian city because whatever I would find out there
beyond the city limits would never be quite as fine.

Well, I didn't believe that for one second. It was like the time
my grandmother took me to a workshop to see how glass was
blown and the adjacent gift shop that sold the little glass
tchotchkes and vases had signs all over that said Don't Touch
the Glass. All I wanted to do was touch that stupid glass, and the
signs made me feel so restricted that I just wanted to break it
all. All the chitchat about how lucky I was to be raised in such a
beautiful neighborhood just made me want to run away and
prove them all wrong. I wanted to bring back the whole world
and drop it on their fuckin' silver platters and say, "See, see what
you stodgy old folks are missing!" But for the time being, I was
ten and it just seemed like a faraway dream.

* * *

Acting classes began early in my family. The rules were simple. Keep everything to yourself. If you have a problem, take care of it on your own. And above all else, have manners. Manners meant that you were well-bred. And breeding was everything in Bloomfield Hills. But manners became particularly handy in front of guests and at all adult gatherings. It was the proof in the pudding. It said that your mother had raised you right and it was a good reflection on the whole family. But all it said to me was that I spent most of my childhood years at the kids' table during these functions and that I was miserable in my too-tight white patent leather Mary Jane shoes from the Easter before, and the Danskin tights, which were always hanging down in the crotch because I was so tall for my age, rubbed against my thighs and made my skin itch. Manners to me always involved some sort of torture. Whether it was the attire we had to wear or the boring events we were expected to attend, all of it seemed like a waste of time. Nevertheless, I had no choice in the matter, so I just went along with it for the most part. It was like make-believe to me. All I had to do was act. Act like I was rich. Act like I was happy. Act like I was well adjusted without a care in the world. These lessons would come in handy down the road.

INT. LADIES' LOUNGE, OAKLAND HILLS COUNTRY CLUB, BLOOMFIELD HILLS, MICHIGAN

MOM
Honey, we don't have all day. Your grandfather is here with some important clients
and we've been in here for twenty minutes.
Now if you're sick, then I'll take you
home.

TOBI

I'm not sick.

MOM

Then what's the problem this time? You
know, you do this every time we go out for
a nice dinner. You eat all the wrong foods
and then we spend half the dinner in the
ladies' room with you sick.

TOBI

I told you, I'm not sick!

MOM

Okay, you're not sick. Then why won't you
come out of the rest room?

TOBI

I'm not gonna tell you 'cause you're just
gonna get mad.

MOM

Yeah, well, I'm gonna get a lot madder if
this takes any longer. Come on, let's go, I
told you everybody is waiting on us at the
table.

TOBI

I don't want to go back there. It's boring.
All there is is old people talking about old
people things and I hate this dress. It's too
small and it's not mine.

MOM

I told you I can't afford to buy you a new
dress this week. Maybe next week we can
go shopping.

TOBI

That's what you always say, but then I
always have to wear hand-me-downs and I
hate them, they're ugly!

MOM

Listen, young lady, you've got about five
more seconds of this before I'm going out
there and making a fool out of you by
telling all those poor people at the table
that we can't have dinner because you
won't leave the rest room. How would you
like me to say that?

TOBI

Fine, I'm coming out, but I'm not going to
talk to those boring people.

MOM

Fine, then just listen. My God, do you think
that for once we could just go out without
having to go through this?

TOBI

Yeah, maybe if we went somewhere where I
liked going.

MOM
And where would that be?

TOBI
Dad's.

From what I gather, when my mother and father split up, I was about two. We moved into my grandparents' home and started our new life. At the time, I didn't know that we had an old life, but apparently we did, or at least I did for a little while anyway, but it didn't sound very exciting living in the poor part of town in a little white house that looks small and gloomy in the Polaroids I've seen. I remember keeping a Polaroid of me and my dad washing the car on a hot summer day and noticing a '67 imprinted on the side white border I had on a shirt with the word "Love" in big mod block letters in primary colors. My hair was cut in a little pageboy with bangs, and I was running and laughing as my dad sprayed me jokingly with the hose. My dad appeared thin and young as he stood by his black Cadillac holding the hose and scrub brush. My brother was also in the picture. He was three years old and washing one of the tires on the car with his little jeans rolled up to his knees. There was a black Australian sheepdog with a white bib of fur around her neck jumping up trying to catch the water coming from the hose. I was told her name was Missy. All I ever knew about my beginning was that Polaroid.

Moving in with my grandparents was a big step up, but for my mother, I'm sure it was a step down. It was 1968, and for the most part all of my mother's friends, including her two sisters, were married. She had two children under the age of two, no job, and no home. Her attempt at starting her own life had faltered. I don't remember the day we moved in, or what month it was, I just remember always living there. This was home to me. This is where my life began.

I loved living with my grandparents. There was always someone around the house, like Clidey the housekeeper, who was family to us. She had children of her own, but they were grown by the time she came to work for us. Her stride confirmed her years of hard work and the strength it took her to rise each day out of bed. Her cleaning was slow and methodical. Her thoughts were the wrinkles on her face. I felt like a spoiled brat around Clidey just living in the house she had to clean. I hated the thought that I got to live in the house and she had to clean it. I didn't understand that. I didn't understand her pain or the quiet stare she gave me when she picked up my scattered toys and dirty clothes. But I loved her. She filled an empty house with life and left me each day with a big hug and a smile. When Clidey was too busy to play jokes on there was also Leonard the gardener. A tall, thin black man from Detroit with a lit Salem always in his mouth and a rake in his hand. Leonard kept to himself most of the time, but occasionally he'd pick up a basketball and shoot some hoops with my brother and me. He mowed, weeded, trimmed the hedges, washed the driveway down with water in the summer and shoveled the snow on the sidewalks in the winter. He'd help me sell lemonade to the golfers that drove down our street on the way to the nine-hole course behind our house. He'd take Twiggy for a walk once and a while, but mostly I was just happy to have someone else around to talk to, and Leonard always had a good "knock knock" joke for me. There were also my grandparents when they weren't traveling. For the most part, there was always something to do or invent. The house provided endless hours of discovery. Room after room was filled with new things to learn about, books to read and pictures to look at. I could spend hours in the library looking at all the old *National Geographic*s and reading cookbooks. My grandmother collected books from everywhere she went and, most of all, the lectures she attended on antiquing and restoration. Her books covered everything from the life of the Amish to the history of the Egyptian pyramids. There wasn't a question I could ask without my grandmother hauling me into the library and pulling down a book.

From there I usually went down the hall to the living room. I loved that room, as it was typically off limits. It had such a proper presence to it. It was the perfect set for my imagination to play princess or any other games where I wanted to be poised and sophisticated. I liked staging my tea parties in there because some of the antiques in that room were petite and made me feel bigger, older. There was also an organ. When my grandmother was in a particularly good mood, she would let me and my brother play on it. Needless to say, we only knew one song: "Chopsticks." After about an hour of that, we were usually shut down. Still, I liked to pretend to play the organ when it wasn't on. Just feeling like an adult in that room made living like a kid easier. As often as I could, I would slip into that room and take off with my dreams. I'd practice sitting up straight on the sofa, holding a teacup in my hand and pretending to be at tea with a bunch of ladies giggling and laughing. I'd walk over to the fireplace mantel and look at the porcelain birds my grandmother collected and touch each one softly so as not to move them an inch. I'd fill the room up with different ladies I had seen with my grandmother when she would host bridge parties. I'd put all the ladies around the room in different chairs and have conversations with them, pretending to be the hostess. I'd talk about a new little "bauble" I had found antiquing, or the roses in my rose garden, and I'd offer them different little cakes and cookies while pouring their tea for them. And before I knew it, hours had gone by and I had lived a whole life in just that one room with me and all the imaginary ladies.

EXT. BLOOMFIELD HILLS HOME, BROOKDALE ROAD
INT. ELEGANT LIVING ROOM

1970s upper-class chic. Simple colors, antiques, handblown glass paperweights, porcelain birds collection, parlor chairs, grandfather clock, organ, silk chartreuse drapes in celery with poly sheers.

TOBI

Oh, Samantha, it's so lovely! How sweet
you were to think of me. What a beautiful
blue jay. I shall cherish this and think of
you every time I look at it.

SAMANTHA
(switching chairs)

Well, really, there is a story behind it, and I
feel I just must tell you the truth. I found
that at the last church rummage sale last
fall when you and I dropped off our things.
Out of the corner of my eye I spotted that
bird! Can you believe it? Of all things, it
was right there sitting on an old box of
books waiting to be checked in. Sure
enough, I went right over while you were

getting the rest of your stuff out of the car,
picked it up and turned it over and I
couldn't believe it. Sure as the day, there
was the Staffordshire stamp with the word
England right underneath. So I marched
that right over to Rose and told her to wrap
it up and that I was going to give it to you
on some rainy day!

TOBI
(switching chairs)
Well, you're a doll to think of me and I'm
glad it rained today!
(Goes over to the fireplace mantel and
places the bird with the others.)
There. That's perfect. Now he's got some
friends.

TOBI
(pretending to hear the doorbell)
That must be the other ladies. Will you
excuse me?

TOBI
Oh, hello, sweetheart. Lovely of you to
come. And who is this?

CYNTHIA
This is my granddaughter, Callie, whom I
brought along for you all to meet. I hope
you don't mind.

TOBI

Oh, don't be silly.

> (putting her hand out to Callie)

How lovely it is to meet you, Callie. Please
come in. Would either of you like some tea?
Clidey, my girl, made some delicious scones
today. Won't you try one? There's blueberry.

CYNTHIA

Oh, really, we shouldn't. We've just lunched
at the Club and you know I'm trying to
watch the ol' waistline. Dick has got me
going to every business dinner in town and
I've put on a few too many pounds. Oh,
but what the heck, just a few bites, right?

TOBI

Well, first I want to start out by thanking
you all for coming out in the rain like this.
God knows we've seen enough of it; however, it's just so good to see you all, rain or
shine. Today, our only matter at hand
before we start our bridge game would be
the Village Women's Club Charity
Christmas Ball. I've been asked to arrange
some of the flowers that will be used to
decorate the main lobby entrance, we still
need volunteers for the other rooms.

SAMANTHA

> (switching chairs)

Oh, listen, darling, I'd do anything for you,

you know I would, but that weekend we're
out of town. Dick has a client that we've
got to visit in Ohio, so I'm so sorry, but I
won't be able to help.

TOBI
(switches chairs)
Quite all right, sweetheart. Don't give it an
extra thought. I just thought I'd mention it.
Maybe next year!
(a loud pounding on the living room door)

GRANDMA
Tobi, are you in there? Come on, dinner has
been ready for fifteen minutes and it's
gonna get cold sitting out there on the
table. Come on, let's go, hurry it up, little
missy! Who were you talking to in there?

Window-shopping was my mother's favorite pastime. Friday night
is when it usually took place, as it was the day my mother got paid.
We would go in to town, usually Birmingham, to admire all the
pretty things as we walked along the street. I don't remember actually going into any of the stores, maybe they were closed, but I do
remember my mother pointing out what she'd buy if she won the
lottery. It was at those times that I realized we were poor. It was difficult to understand how we could live in such a beautiful house
and yet have no money to buy all the accoutrements of wealth.
Those walks gave birth to great fantasies.

I imagined, as my mother held my hand, that one day I would
be the princess in that beautiful dress from Jacobson's department
store, that I could one day buy any dress I wanted and that some-

day we wouldn't just window-shop but actually go into the store and have the salesladies shower us with attention as they introduced the latest fashions. But as I held her hand and we crossed the street, I knew that we were headed home. A home that seemed on loan to me, a place to stay for a while. Somehow, after a few hours of window-shopping, my mother always managed to make me feel as if we had purchased the world. I was tired and exhausted from all the information I had taken in during our shopping trip, as my mother spoke on and on in the car on the way home about the things we would one day buy. I didn't really understand the concept of money then, but I did understand that it could one day buy me those dreams I was painting on the clouds. I also understood that not having money fostered a sense of shame that I was becoming quite accustomed to. These were the years my character and ideals about the world were formed. I saw the world as a place in which I could pretend to be anything. I could pretend to be rich, I could pretend all things in the past never happened, and I could invent my future. I had just learned to pretend to survive, and the only kink as I saw it was that someday, possibly, I could be found out.

EXT. BIRMINGHAM, MICHIGAN—FRIDAY NIGHT
Local clothing shops, gourmet wine and cheese, women's shoes, Crowley's department store, Sander's coffee shop and ice cream, Jacobson's department store.

INT. SANDER'S COFFEE SHOP
Pink and white with a '50s soda shop feel. Brightly lit.
Mom, Tobi and Kane sit at the soda bar and order hot fudge sundaes.

TOBI

Mom, why do we always go window-
shopping on Friday nights?

KANE

Shut up!

TOBI

No, you shut up!

MOM

All right, settle down. Can we just have one
evening without you two fighting? We're
gonna just sit here and finish our sundaes,
then we're gonna go do some window-
shopping. Okay?

KANE

Well, why does she always have to ask such
stupid questions?

TOBI

Why is that such a stupid question? I
wanna know why we never get to go into
those stores and why we just get to look in
the windows.

KANE

'Cause, idiot! We don't have the money to
buy any of those things!

TOBI

Well, why don't we have the money to buy
all those things we see?

KANE

I told you to shut up!

MOM

All right, that's enough. I can't do this anymore. I can't, I just can't. Either the two of
you stop this back and forth or we're going
home.

> (Mom gets up and goes to the ladies'
> room.)

KANE

See, see what you did? You made her upset.
You're so fucking stupid. Don't you know
we don't have any money right now? Don't
you know that Dad never sends us any
money? We window-shop because we're
poor. We're poor, okay? Just accept that.

TOBI

> (crying)

Well, then how can we get more money,
and if we're poor, how come we live in such
a big house?

KANE

We live in a big house because it's not ours,
it's Grandpa's and Grandma's. They just

took us in 'cause Dad left us. So quit
makin' Mom upset asking all those questions, okay?

TOBI

Okay. . .

Mom returns from the ladies' room, wiping the tears from her eyes.

MOM

You kids ready to do some shopping?

TOBI AND KANE

Yeah. . .

KANE

Mom, can I go look in the sporting goods
store window?

MOM

Yes, but meet up back here in twenty
minutes.

Kane runs off to look at the latest hockey gear, and Mom and
Tobi walk toward Jacobson's windows.

MOM

Honey, so you know why we window-shop?

TOBI

Yes.

MOM

Why?

TOBI

Because you want us to dream.

MOM

Yes, that, and I want you to learn by just looking at something, for what it is worth. I want you kids to take a good look at life from the outside before you decide to walk into something you know nothing about. Do you understand? It's not just that we can't afford all these beautiful things, it's just that I want you to understand you don't need all of those things to be happy, that sometimes it's just better to look than it is to buy. . . .

TOBI

(looking in the children's window of
Jacobson's)

See those Danskins over there? I like that color. And see that big white bear on the staircase, the one with the pink bow? I love that bear. He's so pretty. How much do you think that bear is?

MOM

Oh, I don't know, probably a lot! But you know your birthday is coming up, so maybe you can put him on your list.

TOBI

I'm definitely going to. I think I would name him Polar 'cause he's a polar bear.

MOM

Should we go look at the jewelry?

TOBI

Okay.

They walk to Goldman's Jewelry Store.

MOM

See those earrings, those gold hoops in the
back of the case? I love those, they're so
classy. But they're a thousand dollars. I
would love to have those hoops, they're
perfect. What do you think, do you think
they're worth their weight in gold?

TOBI

What do you mean "worth their weight in
gold"?

MOM

I mean, if they were a thousand dollars,
would you pay that if you really loved
them, even though you could probably get
them cheaper at a store that wasn't so
fancy?

TOBI

I think I'd buy them at the cheaper store.

MOM

Exactly. See, that's why we window-shop,
to get the ideas; then if we really like some-

thing we see, we can try to find it cheaper. That's how you shop. Never buy the first thing you see. Always look before you buy, and not just with shopping. With friends, with jobs, with everything you do. Always look at what it is that you want from every angle, then decide if you really need it. Got it, kiddo? . . .

TOBI
Yeah, I got it.

MOM
Look, there's your brother.
(To Kane.)
I've seen that look on your face before. What is it now, what piece of hockey equipment could you possibly not own?

KANE
Will you just come and look.

MOM
Yes, I'll come and look, but I'm just looking.
(She smiles at Tobi.)

Large garbage bags on the doorstep meant the hand-me-downs had arrived from my cousins. I hated the hand-me-downs because they reminded me that we were poor. I hated watching my mother pull out the clothes and try to get me excited as she shuffled through the bags looking for the newer styles and things with the tags still on them. I hated watching my mother's face as she thought of all the beautiful new clothes we had just seen window-shopping and having her feel the shame of not being able to buy them for me. I wondered if she cursed my father in those moments as I threw uncontrollable crying fits about trying on the clothes. I wondered if her insistence upon me picking out things to wear was to give me something to have after all those beautiful clothes we had just seen. Or was it her own unfulfilled dreams that drove her to make me feel pretty? My mother's repeated phrases of inspiration like "It doesn't matter what you wear on the outside, it's what you wear on the inside that counts" only confused me. It was like having a closet full of masks. I really wanted the new clothes in the window, and the old ones just made it worse. But what I wanted more than that was a way in which my mother could give those things to me. I wanted to see her face as she bought those beautiful dresses for me, to see her self-respect as she paid for the dresses. Most of all, I wanted her pain to stop. I wanted her to stop blaming herself for my father walking out. I wanted her to just tell me why he never called on birthdays or Christmas, instead of her trying so desperately to make up for his loss. I wanted her to feel proud of the fact that she was supporting two kids on a hundred dollars a week. I just wanted her to let him go. But she wanted me to feel important, and she wanted me to feel loved. The window-shopping was the education, and the hand-me-downs were the reality, and that was the lesson she was trying to give me. She wanted so desperately to show me the other side of the world that I could someday have, yet she wanted me to know the harsh reality of it as well. I never wore any of the hand-me-downs, but I took a few pieces from the pile each time to make my mother feel better and to accelerate the process of humiliation.

The things we did get to buy with my mother's paycheck were beauty products. Nail polish, mud masks, deep conditioners, and No More Tears detangler for my long, matted hair were at the top of the list. Our bathroom was like a salon. For every new product she bought, I was her guinea pig. She'd say, "Let me try this on you. First you have to wash your face with a cleanser. Never use soap. It will dry out your skin. Always use a cleanser, then, with a hot washcloth, steam your face for two minutes to open up the pores. Always use a washcloth because it acts like an exfoliator on your skin. Then, cleanse, and immediately rinse your face with cold water to close the pores and prevent wrinkles." She spent hours with me in the bathroom, primping and trying out all of her beauty inventions.

She was big on manicures and pedicures. She would put my feet in the sink filled with warm water and a little baby oil and have me soak them for about fifteen minutes. After ten minutes she'd tell me to drop my fingers down into the water and soak my fingernails for the last five minutes. After that, she'd dry me off, sit me in front of the TV, turn on the *Sonny and Cher Show,* and give me a pedicure and a manicure, saying all along, "It's important that you know how to do your own pedicure and manicure, because if someday you don't have the money to get a proper one done in the salon, you can always look as if you've had them done." She thought that if she prepared me in the way of beauty, no matter what else happened, I would always have my looks to rely on. At least that was the message I was getting, and it seemed loud and clear with all the face creams, special brushes and techniques that I was being introduced to, that one day all of this would be important. At ten years old, it just seemed ridiculous.

On the nights when I'd get a pedicure and manicure, I'd sleep with my toes out of the end of the bed and my hands on top of the sheets and close my eyes and hear my mother's voice again with one of her phrases, "No one said that beauty was easy," and with that I was off to sleep.

REAL BLONDES

The big weekend finally arrived. All the whispering on the phone between my mother and father during the previous weeks had resulted in my father and I spending our first weekend alone together. It was a special occasion for me, as I hardly ever saw my father and because when I did spend time with him, every moment seemed like my last. I cherished each second I had with him. It was a chance to discover what all the mystery was about, why my father was considered such a bad guy. I wanted to know why the hushed voices between my grandfather and mother when they spoke of him. Better yet, I wanted to know why they didn't speak of him. It was my big chance to gather more clues about this man that was supposed to be my father.

I waited at the top of the staircase like I always did when someone was supposed to pick me up. From this spot I could see through the porthole window at the bottom of the staircase to the end of the driveway.

I was ready a half hour early. I wanted to make sure that he wouldn't drive off if I wasn't ready in time. I packed my Barbie suitcase with clothes and stuffed my koala bear backpack with my princess matching lime green nightgown and robe and threw it on my back. I tossed my *Young Miss* magazine and a copy of *Cosmo* into the sides of my suitcase, sticking out a little so my dad could notice that I was all grown up and that Mom let me read such cool magazines. I had brushed my hair the night before, a hundred strokes, so it would be extra shiny. Just me and Dad. My brother had some Pee Wee hockey tournament, so he couldn't make it. I was glad. It meant that I got my dad all to myself. My mother did not want to be around when my father picked me up, so she left me with my grandmother. The rules for picking me up were simple. My father was not allowed into the house. Period. The pickup time was 10:00 A.M. on Saturday. I was on the stairs and waiting at 9:30 A.M. I waited for a glimpse of his car to drive up so I could run out and start our journey together. I watched as each car passed by, looking only for the black Cadillac that would deliver my father to me.

I waited until 10:00, until 10:15, until 11:00. I waited, uncomfortable, not moving so as not to wrinkle my dress. I pet Twiggy's head. I heard my grandmother yell up to see if I was still there. I answered reluctantly, flinching at the tone of her voice as she offered to call him to see what had happened. But I refused. "He'll be here," I said. "He's just late."

"Are you sure you don't want me to call?"

"I'm sure. He'll be here." But what that hour and a half late said to me was, I'm not important . . . I'm not good enough for him to be on time . . . he doesn't love me . . . he doesn't even want to pick me up. Each thought of doubt that raced through my head about who I was and what I meant to my father came to me in that hour and a half, and yet I still wanted to protect him, defend him. I still wanted to go away with him for the weekend, and if anything went wrong, all my chances of finding out more about him would be lost forever if he kept screwing up like this. I didn't care that he was hurting me or that I was feeling abandoned. I just wanted him to know he was doing these things. I understood how hard it was for him to be unwelcome by my mother and grandparents; I understood because I was part of him, and the part of him that lived in me also felt uncomfortable driving up that driveway. But I didn't want him to feel shame with me. I just wanted him to feel accepted. I just wanted a dad, whoever the hell he was.

Not a moment before I felt the first tear roll down my cheek, I saw the car. "He's here." "He's here," I yelled out to my grandmother. I picked up my suitcase, kissed Twiggy good-bye and ran outside to meet him. I could see him leaning over to the passenger side to open my door.

> DAD
>
> Hey, little Bogie. Sorry I'm so late. I got
> tied up with a phone call with one of my
> buddies. You know how it is. So it's just
> you and me, kid, for the weekend, huh?

> TOBI
>
> I guess so.

> DAD
>
> What do you say we hit the deli first, get
> ourselves a few sandwiches to go, huh,
> kid?

> V.O.
>
> I remember the red leather interior, his
> black leather blazer, his Marlboro ciga-
> rettes, his slicked-back hair, his crooked
> teeth, his pale skin, the aviator sunglasses,
> his light blue polyester shirt with the collar

out and his black leather short boots with the zipper on the sides. I noticed he had a slight belly but was still tall and lean. I was really just looking for myself in him, but all I could see was him. I needed more time. I needed more time than I was gonna get, so I knew I had to study every detail. I knew that I had to preserve the memories, that I had to watch him, that I had to learn fast, because I was never sure when I'd get the chance to be with him again.

Shopping with my dad in the grocery store was pure excitement. He had talked all the way from my house about what we were gonna buy. Deli food was his favorite. And his favorite deli was Peabody's, a family-owned grocery store in Birmingham that had been around for a hundred years, or at least since my dad was a kid. It was yet another place where my dad had "buddies." He knew the owners, the butcher, said hi to the grocery boys as he walked in. He just liked walking into the place to hear them all say his name in front of his kid. That was it. He loved it. He loved being the hot shot and waving his hand at everybody he knew and having them call out his name.

"Hey, Patrick, how are ya? How's the golf swing?"

"Hey, Patrick, is that your little girl you're always bragging about?"

By the time we finally made our way back to the butcher, I was exhausted from smiling and being dragged all over the store to greet each and every one of them. It was so different than shopping with my grandmother, who barely let me out of the car alone. Most of the time I was told to be quiet while we were shopping or else I wouldn't get to go again, so having a bit of a free-for-all in the grocery store was totally cool with me. I just wanted to make sure I got the pink snowball cakes with the white cream filling into the shopping cart before all my dad's bullshitting was finished.

> PATRICK
> (at the deli)
> So what ya got today? What's fresh? Give
> me what ya got that's fresh. How is the
> roast beef looking? You got some that's
> rare? You know I like it on the rare side,
> but not too pink.

My dad always asked a thousand questions about what he was buying, but he never gave the person he was speaking to a chance to reply. He would just continue on, commenting until his very last question, when he would sort of raise his tone of voice and slam the question right at you.

> PATRICK
> Then give me half a pound of the roast
> beef on the rare side, and what else ya got
> that's fresh? What about these steaks? Hey,
> Bogie, what about you and me grill up
> some steaks tonight and watch the Red
> Wings game? Or maybe the Miss America
> contest, huh? I bet you'd like that? Okay,
> then, Sam, pick me out a couple of nice
> cuts for me and the kid. Looks like we're
> gonna have a barbecue after all. Hey,
> Bogie, run down that aisle and pick us out

some nice baking potatoes and meet me at
the register.

He used to call me Bogie all the time. I guess it was some kind of
golf term or something like that, but I never really understood
why. I was just glad to have a nickname. It was kind of like having a secret code name and I could completely forget my real name.
Besides, I liked my new invented self with my dad. It seemed like
much more fun than just being a kid all the time with my brother
and my mom. And it was so easy to change. All of a sudden I was
free. I wasn't rich, I wasn't poor, I didn't have to have manners, I
didn't have to be quiet, I could just be me. And I had a whole
weekend to be just that.

After the clerk rang up all the groceries and told my father how
much the bill had come to, my father went into the second half of
his show. I had seen him do it a couple times before, but every time
I was with him I waited on pins and needles as he'd open his wal-
let to look for some cash to pay.

PATRICK
Hey, Jimmy, looks like I'm a little short
today. You know I'm good for it, right?
Come on, I got the kid with me today. I'll
catch up with you next week, okay?

That was the game. By the time he finished bullshitting with all
of them for the half hour we had been in the store, asking about
all their wives and showing me off, they were too embarrassed
to say no. They just let him slide. But I couldn't figure out why
we had to do so much work in the store just to tell them we
couldn't afford to pay, and if we couldn't afford to pay, then
why all the big shot gestures and smiles and hugs? What did all

that mean? Well, it meant selling. And selling was the name of the game. That's how he operated everywhere he went. Always the salesman, he worked on the buddy system. He used to say all the time, "Oh, I got a buddy here, I got a buddy there, I got a buddy that will fix that for you, I got a buddy that will help you out with that." You name it, he had a buddy for ya. And if he didn't have a buddy there, we didn't go there. So I just figured if ya didn't have one of those buddies wherever you went, there was just no point in going there. 'Cause if ya didn't have a buddy where you were going, you couldn't get stuff for free. It seemed like a pretty simple game to me. All you had to do was have lots of buddies.

PATRICK
So, kiddo, we got what we needed, right?

Right then and there I had learned to lie, bullshit, pretend, sell, act, and every other tool on earth that I would need to get what I wanted by just learning how to persuade that person right in front of me to do what I needed them to do. I also learned in that moment not to feel remorse. We laughed in the car all the way home, eating deli slices and drinking Vernor's.

INT. PATRICK'S CONDO, BIRMINGHAM, MICHIGAN
Two-bedroom apartment, '70s yellow mustard color palette,
a plaid couch in the living room, a new color TV, Formica
kitchen table with vinyl chairs in the dining room with
wall-to-wall shag carpeting.

PATRICK
So, Bogie, what's it gonna be? The Red
Wings or Miss America?

TOBI

Miss America!

PATRICK

Okay, kiddo. Miss America it is. You find
the channel and I'll go and throw the steaks
on the grill. And would you grab a cold
Budweiser out of the icebox for your dad
and bring it outside to me?

TOBI

Sure.

EXT. CONDO COMMUNITY GRILL AREA

Patrick goes outside with the steaks and heads toward the grill.
Tobi channel surfs until she catches the previews for Miss
America. Tobi goes into the kitchen, opens a Budweiser, and
heads out toward the grill. She sees Patrick speaking to a tall,
beautiful blonde woman. The woman seems upset and is waving her hands in the air. Tobi ducks out of sight and moves
closer to eavesdrop.

PATRICK

I told you my kid is here for the weekend
and I can't introduce you to her, it's just not
the right time. . . .

BLONDE WOMAN

It's never the right time, is it, Patrick? I
mean, when the hell is it gonna be the right
time? When are you gonna tell them that
you've got a girlfriend, for Christ's sake?

We've been together for two fucking years.
You'd think by now you could let them
know.

PATRICK

Listen, I can't tell her now, okay? It's not
right, for Christ's sake. She barely knows me
and I'm not gonna just lay that on her. I told
you, honey, when the time is right I'll tell
them both, but not until the time is right.

BLONDE WOMAN

Well, I don't know if I can wait that long,
you know, I've got my life too. I can't just
wait around for you to decide to get your
shit together. I mean, I deserve more than
that. What the hell do you think I've been
sticking with you for? Well, I'll tell you
what for, I want'a get married, that's what
for, and I think you owe me that for being
so patient.

PATRICK

Honey, I told you, I can't talk about this
now. Tobi is inside and she's coming out
with my beer and I don't want her to see us
out here talking like this. I've got enough
problems with her mother as it is,
okay? . . .

Patrick leans over, gives Blonde Woman a kiss and slaps her on
the butt. Blonde Woman leaves. Tobi watches quietly from
behind a fence, sneaking peeks through the slats.

PATRICK

Hey, kiddo, thanks for the Bud. Did you
find the Miss America channel?

TOBI

Yeah. Who was that lady that you were
speaking with?

PATRICK

Oh, she's one of my neighbors. That's
Cheryl. Maybe you two can meet some
time. I told her all about you and your
gymnastics.

Tobi looks down at the ground while Patrick speaks on and on
about what he has told Blonde Woman about her. Tobi's dream
of her parents ever getting back together seems to be getting
further and further away.

PATRICK

So, kiddo, it's just you and me tonight and
Miss America! Hey, maybe one day you'll
be Miss America, huh? Yeah, maybe one
day I'll see you on TV and say, "That's my
little Bogie . . ."

TOBI

Yep, I could be Miss America if I wanted to
be, and you know what my talent would
be? Gymnastics. But do Miss Americas have
to be blonde or can they have brown hair?

PATRICK
Why do you ask that question?

TOBI
Because that woman you were speaking
with looked like a Miss America, and she
was blonde.

PATRICK
Oh, no, honey. She just dyes her hair
blonde. All those Miss Americas are real
blondes.

FAST CASH AND QUICK MONEY

My situation had escalated to an unbearable state of poverty and humiliation. All opportunities for modeling were gone, and the possibility of becoming an actress was looking even less promising, so I was forced to face facts. Either go home to Florida, where my mother was now living since my father had left her for the second time, and start life over, or continue on in L.A. trying to find work and keep a hopeful attitude toward my future as an actress. My situation was bleak. I was three months behind in rent, four months behind in car payments, no health insurance, no car insurance, and, worst of all, my cash was running out. I had made up my mind that I still wanted to live in L.A., but I would have to find a real job. Sure, I was always filling out applications whenever I went out at night and sometimes during the day, but for the most part I didn't want any of those hideous jobs like waitressing or bartending or hostessing or working in a clothing store. I just wanted to support my habit of staying out all night and going to clubs, and I wanted to figure out how to do that without actually getting one of those jobs.

That was what was going on in my head at the time I reconnected with Steven Ashley. Steven Ashley can best be described as the premier Doorman of the '80s. He had survived Studio 54 and outlived its owners. He was somewhat famous, mysterious and shy. Yet he could be direct and to the point when it came time to say no. Steven Ashley had made himself a success by saying no to thousands of the famous and the infamous. He was what every club owner dreamed of in a Doorman. He could make or break your club in one weekend. Everyone who was anyone in the business knew of or had heard of Steven Ashley. Burned out on New York, he'd sought refuge in Los Angeles, hoping to open his own private bar.

I had heard through my club brat friends that some New Yorkers were building a bar over on Melrose Avenue and I had driven by a couple of times during the day, thinking that I might run into someone I knew. I had been told they were looking for waitresses and hostesses from New York. So I figured if I just drove by and dropped in I might be able to fill out an application or do some talking with the owners to see if I could get a job.

But it's what I had to face in the car before I went into the bar that was most difficult for me. I knew I ran the risk of running into someone I knew from the New York club scene, and I felt humiliated. I had once been a New York model. I had had movie stars for boyfriends. I had run around in limos and eaten at the best restaurants and shopped at the most expensive stores, and now I was outside on the street in my Toyota Corolla that I couldn't even pay for, hustling for a waitressing job. I couldn't even believe that the nightmare I was living had actually come true. Why had I bet it all on my looks? Why had I given the best years of my modeling career over to some fuckin' brat-packer actor—why? How could I have been so stupid, and why did I need to go on in this madness anymore, this charade of a town filled with all these promises of stardom and money and success? Why?

I didn't want to cry in the car again like I did so often, but every time I tried not to think about what could have been, or what should have happened in my life, the tears would just well up and I would drop my head down and let them fall. The idea of pushing myself another inch just to get from one place to the next was destroying me. I thought if I walk into that bar and ask for a job, then have I failed? Have I truly failed? Will this mean that it's over for me, that I'm just like everybody else? That I'm not special, not talented, not smart? Is that what this means? Or does it mean that I surrender to who I am today? That I say whatever has been in my past and whatever will lie in my future I will accept. Because if I walk in that bar and they do recognize me from New York and then ask me the dreaded question, Why do you need a waitressing job? and I answer, Because I need the money, I think to myself, then will all the pretending be over for me? Will all the role-playing and bullshitting about who I really am be over if I can humble myself to ask for this job? Or will I stay in my car and look into the rearview mirror and just watch the tears fall down? What's it gonna be? That's when the answer came. It's gonna be about me . . . it's all gonna be about me from this point on, I'm taking control. There's not gonna be any wishing or hoping that things turn out okay, or thinking that some white and shining prince is gonna save me. No, I'm sick of that shit! From now on, I'm taking control. I'm the one who calls the shots in my life. I'm the one who takes care of me. And I'm gonna go in that fuckin' bar, and with whatever it takes I'm gonna ask them for a job. That's it. No more shame. I'm tired of shame. I need a goddamn job. Fuck it! I'm getting out of this hideous car and I'm gonna change my life. I'm not a prima donna anymore. That's all it took. A little chat with myself in the car, and I was ready.

That was the day I became a survivor. When I looked back into the mirror to wipe the tears from my eyes, I saw that they had vanished. I had wiped away all the pain and memories of the past.

Everything I had worked for, everything I had earned was gone. It was a new me. I couldn't shed tears for my past regrets and things that never were. I had to survive. I had to eat. I was looking through a new set of eyes. My new eyes would see no shame in lying. They would see no boundaries in getting from one place to the next. I was free to judge, free to discriminate, and free from anything that would hold me back from getting what I wanted. There was no longer a right way or a wrong way to the way I was going to be living. It's just the way things were gonna be.

The bar looked like nothing from the street. The address I had been given was above an old heavy wooden door, and there was nothing else to the building except one window that had been blacked out from the inside. I went over and over again in my mind the address on the slip of paper to make sure I had not reversed the numbers and arrived at the wrong address, like I had done so many times in my life. I knocked quietly on the door and waited. I knocked again. I pounded as hard as I could and there was still no answer.

I thought to myself, How could I have done this again? Not this fuckin' time, goddamn it. How could I have fucked up again? These stupid numbers, shit! Okay, fuck it! Never mind, it was not meant to be, and I can't even remember which club brat gave me the fuckin' address to even call. Shit, I hate this day, it sucks. Just as I was walking away, someone called.

STEVEN

Hey, Tobs.

TOBI

Holy shit! No way! Not you! This is your club?

                    STEVEN
It's mine.

                     TOBI
Oh my God! When did you get to this shit
hole of glamour?

                    STEVEN
Oh, I've been here for about two years.

                     TOBI
Yeah? Two fuckin' years and now this? A
club?

                    STEVEN
Why?

                     TOBI
Fuck, never mind, it's good to see you.

                    STEVEN
It's good to see you too. Want a beer?

                     TOBI
Of course I want a beer. So what's up with
this place? Is it yours?

                    STEVEN
Yeah, mostly. I have a partner, but for the
most part it's mine.

                    TOBI
So you did it, you got your own place.

                    STEVEN
Yeah, I did it. It's a fuckin' bitch, though.
We're doing it mostly ourselves. Come on
in, I'll show you around.

The first thing I noticed about the space was the bar. It was one of
those dark, mahogany bars that looked like it had been there for a
hundred years. It ran along the whole side of the wall down
toward the front door. Behind the bar were mirrors divided by
thick English scrolled molding. The shelves behind the bar were
empty. Looking around I noticed the old cash register, the tip glass,
I took in the smoky smell of the room that seemed to be locked in
the walls forever and the old red carpet stained with memories of
years gone by. Then I rested myself on a stool, leaned my elbows
on the bar and inhaled. I inhaled it all. All the dampness of the spilt
beers, all the half-dried ashtrays, the dingy bar back cloths, the
wash bins, the rinse bins, and the half-empty whiskey bottle that
sat alone behind the bar. I had finally found my home. I loved
every one of those smells. They were like chicken noodle soup to a
sick child. I had found my cure.

                    TOBI
So, listen, Steven, I came by because I need
a job.

                    STEVEN
What kind of job?

TOBI

I don't know, maybe a bartender, or hostess,
whatever you got.

STEVEN

Well, I don't have anything now, but
maybe after we open I can get you a few
shifts hostessing, okay?

TOBI

Okay, listen, it was great seeing you, good
luck with this place.

STEVEN

Tobs, yeah! We'll talk soon, okay?

TOBI

Okay, take care.

STEVEN

You too.

The steps I took that led out onto the street were in slow motion.
With each one I felt like I had never walked a day in my life. I let
the weight of my motorcycle boots carry me toward my car. I
pulled my sunglasses out of my purse and put them on to guard my
eyes from the blinding California light. I could still taste the beer
on my tongue as I searched for my keys in the pockets of my black
leather jacket. I noticed my faded jeans with the worn and
restitched patches on the knees, but I couldn't remember exactly
what day it was, mostly I think because it didn't really matter to
me; they all seemed the same anyway. Sunny, bright, and beautiful.

Just like those stupid postcards from the head shops on Hollywood Boulevard. "Live it up in sunny California," on top of some cheesy picture of a girl or guy in a G-string running down the beach. The only thing I ever saw on a postcard in Michigan was either a picture of a deer during hunting season or the Great Lakes, and neither one of those was sticking in my head like the bare bottoms on the beach. One thing I knew for sure was that my version of California and the one on the postcards were going to be quite different, and they were going to be different starting that day I walked out of the bar, smelling of smoke and beer at eleven o'clock in the morning and loving it.

EXT. STUDIO CITY GUESTHOUSE—DAY

> **TOBI**
> If I can somehow come up with the rent in
> the next two weeks, will you let me stay?

> **LANDLORD**
> Yes, of course, but this is getting a little
> scary for me and my wife. I mean, we
> really need the money and if you can't
> come up with some of the rent, then we'll
> have to ask you to leave.

That was the conversation prior to the phone ringing, along with the other threatening phone calls from bill collectors and repo companies asking the whereabouts of my car at all times, should they need to pick it up for defaulting on the loan, as well as the phone company, the cable company, the gas company, and the one department store credit card I had, on which I used to charge big-ticket items like televisions and stereo equipment so I could pawn them for cash down the road if I was short on money. I just figured that there was only one reason to charge something and that was to resell it. It seemed simple to me. Anything that could be turned into cash equaled staying in Los Angeles. It was always about staying in L.A no matter what the cost. I figured that if I could survive long enough, I'd find that pot of gold. I just needed to buy myself some time to figure out how I was gonna get it, along with all those promises. The promises were things that I invented in my head. They were the things that I saw through the windows as I strolled down Rodeo Drive or the beautiful black, shining cars that passed me all day long on the streets, or the big, beautiful homes that lined Beverly Drive, the things I saw when I was a little girl window-shopping with my mother in Birmingham. They were all just things that I saw through that same window, all the things I couldn't have. The promises were all about things that I could someday have, when I got rich and famous. I wasn't seven years old, holding my mother's hand, listening to her dreams for me. I was twenty-four and still looking through that same window and standing out on the outside, afraid to go in and buy it for fear that they'd find out I really couldn't afford it, or more importantly, that I wasn't who I said I was, that I was still lying, still trying to be the little rich girl.

THE PRIVATE LINE

The worst thing I could have imagined happening to me, was happening. My plan to move to Los Angeles and become a famous actress was failing. Worse, I wasn't even getting the chance to fail. With one B movie and a couple of embarrassing plays way off, three thousand miles away from Broadway, I lacked confidence in it ever materializing into anything other than a job occupation I threw around in conversation. Sure, I had all the right training from the best acting schools in New York and Los Angeles, plus the ones I lied about on my resume, but actually getting an agent and surviving the bullshit of the business was beneath me. I mean, all my friends, at least the ones I had slept with, were actors and very successful, so it made no sense to me that I should have to grovel around town, sending out headshots and resumes, meeting with low-life C-level agents when I figured I'd given half these fuckin' actors most of my compelling stories, which were somehow ending up in their films by apparent osmosis. The whole acting gig was totally confusing to me, and it offered such little rewards that the only thing good about it was this wonderful luxury to say that you were an actor, which meant that you were either beautiful and talented, or one of the other of those two, or you were truly an actor. But the title also meant two other very important things. Famous or not famous. Rich or poor. I mean, I can describe it many ways, this actor term. But at the end of the day if you're not getting paid for it, you're not doing it. And I sure as fuck wasn't getting paid for it, but I seemed to be doing a lot of it, so I decided to use my label at any opportune time, like parties or bars or restaurants, just to compensate for my inadequate existence as an unemployed actress. But at the same time it was a perfect cover-up for what I was actually after. My story. I wanted the skinny on everything and everybody. Not because I wanted to use it against anybody, but I was driven to find my story. I wanted to understand how someone could build a career from the ground up and struggle to obtain success, and then, in turn, piss it all away on drugs or whatever they could find to destroy the opportunity they had been given. I was really chasing the best story of fame I could find. I wanted to know how it applied to everything and everybody I seemed to come in contact with, including myself. But for the most part, actors made the best specimens, so what better way to attract an actor than to become one. I totally believed in the theory of becoming what you wanted to be or study, and it seemed to be working in Los Angeles. As far as I could see, the plan was well in gear long before I arrived; I felt I was merely hopping on the train with everybody else. I figured that all this research I wanted to do so desperately must have a reason, but early on the only drawback to living this interesting and somewhat shallow life of research was that I wasn't getting paid.

V.O. NARRATOR
I made a vow to find my own story, meet
my own characters, find a few locations
where the story would take place, research
the characters that would move the story

forward, find a thought-provoking place for
the narrator (me) to live, work, eat, hang
out. Really, I could include anything I liked
doing on a day-to-day basis in my story.
Those were my rules. I thought of a few
friends I knew who would appear in my
story. The rest of the characters I would
meet along the way.

There was **Charlotte,** A Jesus freak who would fail to lead me to
Christ but who would save my soul. Anyway, she was a beautiful,
tall, slender brunette. We met in acting class. She was the only non-
Hollywood friend I had. She would later become the only true friend
I had ever known. I would teach Charlotte about Hollywood and
she would teach me psalms. I would smoke pot and drink beers when
we went out, Charlotte would order Perrier and write down passages
from the Bible on cocktail napkins. We had nothing in common.

There was **Stella,** whom I met at **Stella's** nightclub a few days
after arriving in Los Angeles. No one introduced us, we simply met
that first night I came to her club. She noticed that I was alone and
asked me in her husky Greek voice who I was with. I told her no
one, and she grabbed my hand and marched me over to table 8,
where she regularly sat Jack, Sean, Marlon and all the other one-
name superstars. When we arrived at the table she lit a cigarette
and flipped her long, shiny black hair away from her face and said,
"There you go, kid, now you're not alone." I was her empty seat
filler. I didn't care. Every Saturday I sat next to the most exciting
actors, directors, producers, writers one can meet. I never ques-
tioned why she was helping me, I just showed up on Saturday
nights, sat at table 8 and waited for the other guests to arrive. After
a few months of this we started hanging out at her house in the
Hollywood Hills. We smoked pot, cooked, read to each other, and

helped each other along the way. Stella was always half naked. She hated clothes. She was always hot, even in the winter, and was completely comfortable hanging around the house in a sexy little teddy or negligee. She was my mentor, my introduction to Hollywood, and my best friend.

*Then there was **Henry**, my lover. He was perfectly complicated, beautiful, intelligent, childish, sexy, and a bit dirty. Essentially homeless, he spent his time moving from one hotel to the next. He was well traveled, well read, recited Shakespeare soliloquies in bed to me, rode motorcycles, crashed them, had excellent manners and the stance of a prince. When he spoke, he made large, sweeping movements with his hands to illustrate events that had taken place in his day. He was an actor, a musician, and an excellent lover. He was successful, famous, rich, and emotionally unavailable. He was perfect for me. I could hide in Henry, make believe with Henry, fall in love with Henry. Then he would disappear for months. We were only lovers. We had no commitment, no rules, only an agreement to be what we needed to each other at those moments when we were together. No time passed between us. We took up each time where we had previously left off. We didn't discuss lost time, we didn't discuss the future, we just stayed in the moment. Henry was everything to me. I loved him. I just couldn't tell him that.*

V.O. NARRATOR

I was sick of being me. No money, no job, no boyfriend, always moving from place to place. I needed a break, so I figured until one came along I'd just pretend to star in my own story. That way all the crazy shit that was happening to me would be meaningful. For example, if I was evicted, lost my job, got arrested, couldn't pay my bills, lied all the time, all of it would enrich my story. By thinking about all these negative things as dramatic material, I could see them in a positive light. I really had just one goal in mind: To find myself. To find out who I was, who I was supposed to be, what I was supposed to do and whom I was supposed to love. I set out on a journey to become the author of my own story.

I made my usual Sunday night list of my good and bad qualities.

Good things about me
Beautiful
Funny
Loving
A good friend

Bad things about me
Depressed
Moody
Coldhearted
Tough

Things I need to quit
Smoking   Swearing
Drinking   Lying
Blow jobs
Sugar
Salt

By Monday, I'd already forgotten the list and tripped out the door with bells on my toes toward the nearest bar and the fastest way to use my actress label to begin researching my story. Oh, the rush of good navigation!

V.O. NARRATOR
I'm about to meet Klaus Van Dern, one of

71

Hollywood's hottest action directors.
Viking-like, he's hard to miss. He stands
6'4" and has a dirty blonde '90s-type
ponytail. He's single, always drunk on
vodka, incredibly successful, sexy, and
from a conversational standpoint, stupid.
My goal for the evening is to try and
hook up with him. I plan on giving him a
blow job. Fucking him at this point seems
out of the question. I need a director for
my story. I don't have one yet. I've read
about him in the trades. For sure I'll
remind him of his maiden Icelandic babes
back home. I'll choose a more Swedish
approach to my look for the evening.
Straight blonde hair and simple, natural
makeup.

The Roxbury, centrally located on Sunset Strip, was "the club at
which to be seen," but for me it was the opposite. I felt it said all
the wrong things about me. If you were the type to go to the
Roxbury, then you definitely weren't the type for me. I hated big
clubs. There was less of a chance to hook up with my research subject for the night. However, there were exceptions to the rules.
Tonight's exception was Klaus Van Dern.

I was invited to a cast and crew party for the latest summer
blockbuster. I'm sure on some previous night I had hooked up with
somebody in order to get me there. It was part of the game.
Befriending one to get to another was an easy way around a lot of
corners in Hollywood. It cut through the red tape. Picking my
allies was a calculated task, their perceived value to my story the
criterion. Separating those who could further my research from

those who could not was a pastime for me. I determined the value of your friendship by how well you were connected and your flexibility as a game player: i.e., were you on the studio list for invites to premiere parties; could you call the Ivy last minute on a Saturday night and get a table for six; or who was your crew, who were your close circle of friends and the ones you only saw on special occasions; could you get me into the Vanity Fair party after the Oscars; or better yet, could you get me closer to whomever it was I wanted to sleep with that week. My favorite words were "Let me introduce you to a friend of mine." Like giving a little girl candy.

As always, I had done my research before meeting my Director. I had read the trades, checked Army's column, and dabbled in the rags, but I never considered them a thorough source of information. It was just for the pictures and a general overview. So by the time I was introduced to my Director, I had something to say other than "Hey, congratulations on your movie." My technique never varied. Make eye contact as I introduce myself and say my name. "Is that your real name?" "No, Tobi is just a nickname for Tobin." "What's your real name?" "It doesn't matter." It was like catching frogs by the pond. I'd just wait for them to jump, put them in my pocket.

I don't think it hurt that I was beautiful, but I knew I needed more than beauty to make it home with him. After the name game was over, I waved back to my "ride" and drifted over to him, turning my back to my Director. The chase was on. The Director has to find a way to my "ride" to get the scoop on me. Who do I know? This determined whether I was safe, which, in "Hollywood Gabber," is, Can I actually fuck this girl and know that she won't run and tell? Without fail I'd pass. Who knows what names my "ride" would drop? Who gave a shit? This was my story.

After my "ride" had confirmed to me that my Director wanted to have a little after-hours soiree at his Hollywood Hills party pad,

I was in business. There was just one step that I couldn't fuck up; the casual brush-off of the "ride." I had to be careful. He too was connected, and maybe I'd need him again for another "ride." I hated this part of the game with a passion. It was so cruel. I felt guilty for robbing one soul to get another, knowing my "ride" wanted me too. He was the guy who never got the girl. Conversely, however, he was also the guy who found the girl for the Director, so he was covered. We all were. It was a food chain. Find your food or starve.

The next step was leaving the club separately so that no one could bust us together. I wasn't interested in fame, I was interested in information, so I was always the one to initiate the "back door exit." It worked to my advantage. It assured my prey that I could be trusted. I walked to the corner of Sunset by the Chateau Marmont and had him pick me up beneath the Marlboro Man. We were off, headed up Laurel Canyon to Mulholland Drive, another quick left and up a steep hill, and there she sat, the party pad. They all looked the same to me after a while, Frank Lloyd Wright–inspired architecture, Michael Smith interiors, Bose sound system, gardenia-scented candles from Illume, and of course the dogs. . . . What kind of dogs my prey owned always interested me, not only because I love dogs but because I was dying for one and everyone in Los Angeles seemed to have one except me.

After I bonded with the four Great Danes, I moved on to him. The party pad was in full romantic bloom. While I was bonding, he was taking care of business—setting the lights low, illuminating the pool, lighting candles, pulling a bottle of Cristall from the refrigerator as he feigned a look of surprise and asked if I would care for some. I wanted to say, "Skip the bullshit, fucker, let's get on with it." Basically, I wanted all the details about his character, where he lived, what kind of car he drove, who his friends were and how good a lover he was. Then, I was ready to move on. But first, it was time to pay for the information. However, there was always a chance that maybe, he would be the one. You know, the One. The one that really sees you. The one that really finds you interesting and wants to know you better. Maybe, just maybe, he'll like me. That's how it went in my head. That's what I thought every time I fucked somebody for the story, because if I hadn't had the story or the research, I couldn't have done it. By my own rules I could do whatever with whomever I chose until I met the one that would make me stop.

All the steps from here on in were by rote. Just follow his lead. Let him draw the bath and dim the lights. Wait for him to toss me a white terry-cloth robe just like his. It's my turn to strip. He's already naked in the tub waiting. Well, I sure as fuck don't need to give him a show. For what—a part in one of his movies? Get real. I never fell for that. I was way past that dream. But that's why he thought I was there. What a sucker. How many times did I have to be told you can't fuck for roles, you just can't . . . but you know what? I didn't really believe that. I just thought it was all a numbers game. "What beautiful tits you have."

"Thanks," I replied and got into the sudsy tub. Champagne in hand, I swirled around naked, my blonde hair tousled on top of my head, and, laughing, blew bubbles at him.

It was all the same to me. The same bed with the same view, just a different director with a different cock. I tried for the quickie blow job to hurry my after-hours exit, but sometimes it failed. This time, after all was said and done, the same words came floating over to my side of the bed: "Darling, let's just keep this between you and I." Okay, fucker, I thought to myself, except for that book I may one day write . . . well, I guess you're not the one anyway.

I managed to sleep some until morning, when I was awakened by the phone call that always came on weekday mornings with my prey—some studio fuck wanting some meeting or whatever, some assistant wanting to confirm flight information or whatever, just the fuckin' phone ringing and reminding me it was another weekday with no job and nothing but the evening to look forward to. I rolled over and glanced at my Director to retrieve those beautiful words I'd hear every morning I was on the run, waiting for them like a puppy on its hind legs, paws up. "You look so beautiful in the morning."

That was my cue. It was time to get cab fare.

INT. HOLLYWOOD HILLS HOME—LIVING ROOM

White couches, modern, sleek, a Blue Dog painting. Tobi is dressed and waiting for the cab to come. She speaks with the maid, while the Director gets dressed.

> MAID
> So, young lady, would you like some fresh juice while you wait for your ride?

> TOBI
> Oh yes, my ride, well actually, my ride is already home.

> MAID
> Excuse me?

> TOBI
> Oh, nothing, I'm sorry, I was just thinking out loud. Yes, juice would be great.

> MAID
> You know, those four big dogs of his almost pushed me into the pool this morning. Why, I say to him, do you have dogs, why? And so big, I say, why not you have four small

dogs? And you know what he says to me,
pretty lady? He says, because I have you,
Emerita. So there, you see, because he has
me to clean the house, feed the dogs and
wash his clothes, he doesn't need a bride.
But still he doesn't listen. So I say . . . uh,
oh well, it just my job. But a pretty lady like
you should have somebody that loves you
and wants to have you as his wife. . . .

The maid hands Tobi a glass and continues to clean the house
as Mr. Director sashays down the steps, adjusting his Cartier
and checking the battery on his cell phone.

DIRECTOR

So, my Swedish berry, cab come?

TOBI

No, I was just waiting here and speaking
with Emerita.

DIRECTOR

Ah, so you met. Yes, what would I do without my Emerita.

TOBI

Well, according to Emerita, you'd probably
get married.

DIRECTOR

Oh, is that what you two were giggling about
down here—me? Yes, well, she's probably
right, so maybe I should marry you.

TOBI
(jokingly)
But darling, we only just met. And besides,
I don't cook, clean or do laundry, so you
better stick with Emerita.

A loud beeping is heard from the driveway.

TOBI
Oh, that's me . . . saved by the bell. So,
sweets, can you lend me a few for the fare?

DIRECTOR
Oh, of course, sorry you had to ask. I'm
rushing, and I've lost my manners.

TOBI
Oh, no, I think we both lost those last
night . . . so big kiss, I left my number on
your nightstand. You know, just in case you
miss me.

Tobi gives him a peck on the cheek and waves good-bye to
Emerita, barrels her way past the Great Danes and the pool,
descends two flights down to the driveway, and is greeted by a
Pakistani cabbie standing next to the cab with the rear passenger door open.

CABDRIVER
So we go?

TOBI
To Studio City, right down the hill, it's not
far at all. Can I smoke?

CABDRIVER
Maybe? What you want to smoke?

TOBI
A cigarette, just a cigarette.

CABDRIVER
Okay, you smoke a cigarette, I smoke a
cigarette, but it's early you know, not so
healthy for us to smoke so early, right?

TOBI
Yes, you're right.
Tobi rolls down her window and lights her cigarette.

TOBI
You know what I wish? I wish it would
always stay dark. I find the light so blinding.
I feel naked in the light.

CABDRIVER
What did you say? Did you say you are
naked? Because I can't have you naked in
my cab, lady.
(He waves his finger.)

TOBI
No, I said I feel naked by the sun, I'm not
naked now. I just want to go home . . .

CABDRIVER
Where is home, what is street address?

Tobi is overtired, and the street numbers of her address are getting reversed in her head. Her dyslexia is kicking in. She takes a moment to breathe deeply.

TOBI

It's 4809 Sunshine Terrace. Yes, four eight zero nine.

The cab arrives at her house.

CABDRIVER

Ah, thank you so much for the tip, a pretty lady like you not married, what a shame.

Tobi takes a moment before getting out of the cab. She thinks about what he has said.

TOBI

I bet you say that to all the girls you pick up at that house?

CABDRIVER

I do . . .   (Laughs)

The Tuesday morning that followed a night of story chasing came too quickly. Upon awakening for the second time, this time in my own bed, the sight of my telephone cords ripped from the phone jacks and hurled across the room reminded me of the all-too-confusing state of peace I had sought when I'd arrived home. They represented the information lines to my life and the ongoing character I had created. Separated by two phone lines, my life separated itself. The public line being for anyone and everyone I met, and the private line being for a few close friends and Henry. Through these two lines or lives, I communicated. Determining my state of mind, I decided which line to plug back in. Not only were the two lines a separation of lives, they facilitated the separation of lies; that made up the character of me. Prior to having two telephone lines, the possibility of getting caught in a lie had been pretty damn good. By separating the lives I could control my behavior and lead a perfectly fulfilling life, both in story and reality.

So deciding which, if either, to plug in seemed like the only decision upon awakening, besides what to eat and when to shower or not. I enjoyed feeling grungy on the outside, as that was how I felt internally. It might let others know the pain I was feeling, and maybe they would see a sign and save me. Unfortunately, grung chic had hit Los Angeles pretty hard, and the only thing my friends noticed about me during this state was how terribly fashion conscious I was.

The smell of my skin and the club stamps all over my hand from the night before reminded me of the various moments I was trying to escape, the hell that faced me in the daylight hours. I felt reassured by my dirty jeans and my flannel shirt. By choosing the clothes from the evening before, I could avoid my closet and the potential to set off a most unwanted panic attack. Many hours of the day would have to go by before I could consider the dreaded closet and what decisions lay there for me. I was naked in the morning. I was without a face to hide behind or a character to play, and dressing that naked girl without even knowing who she was or what she wore was like shopping for a gift for someone you don't know, so it just seemed easier to slip into the girl from the night before and hope for the best.

Driving around Los Angeles in the daylight, unemployed, was hideous. The thought of actually looking for a job was humiliating. The very pursuit of it offered nothing more than repeated disappointments and a clear vision of what my life had become.

I started making yet another one of my lists, titled Finding a Job. Under that heading I listed all the things that I could use to beat the system and find employment. The first thing under that title was beauty. Of course I knew it was the most obvious, but it was also the most effective. The second was intellect, this being the most powerful tool, and the most effective for navigating through all the Hollywood bullshit. Last but not least was connections. This included all persons involved, from the valet parkers to the heads of studios, because the name of the game was still how to cut corners and enter Hollywood through the kitchen door. I knew there was some price to pay, but whatever . . .

To accomplish this task meant the "party girl" hat would have to go on, thus ensuring many nights before me of meeting, greeting, wining and dining, and the occasional late night at a producer's house or actor's hotel room, but it all seemed so exciting that the possibility of getting hurt in the process didn't occur to me. The only price that I could see was keeping all the secrets inside and not having anyone to share them with. I figured the other part of my meager life that existed in reality would sooner or later catch on to my new invented self and everything would work out in the end.

Filling my daylight hours in order to appear as though I was actually trying to find a job became a challenge. After hitting the local coffee shop until 11:30 in the morning and reading all that *Drama-Logue* had to offer in the way of student films and ridiculous auditions, I was lost. I had one of two choices: Go shopping or look for work. Shopping had become my favorite pastime in Los Angeles, not to mention all the information I was collecting for my story. It seemed every shopkeeper in Los Angeles was eager to share some random celebrity anecdote. I quickly became familiar with how diseased in celebrity gossip these establishments were. I was curious how far they would go in relinquishing all the information I was so interested in hearing. My favorite stores were antique stores and the all-too-familiar "shabby chic" type of stores. I loved, too, those stores that had pictures of the owners with all their celebrity customers holding big shopping bags with the store's name on them like they had just looted the place. It was endless, the amount of information that I could get from these places. I found out what new restaurants had opened, what new clubs were hot, who was dating who, who had come in last week with whom, what size they were wearing, what colors they liked, where they lived, what movie they were shooting. It was better than the *Hollywood Reporter.*

The other places that I would look for a job and do story research were, of course, bars and clubs. I preferred bars to clubs, especially on the off nights, like Sunday. It made my research easier. By actually seeing these people in action I was able to learn so much more than I could through gossip. And for the most part, the kind of folks I was looking for weren't out on the weekends, so my schedule became Sunday through Thursday, unless, of course, there was a party. In that case I would skip the bars altogether and work the party. It was at this time that I discovered my fondness for bars. Oh, what glorious places. Always dark, always full of liquor, always open, and always glad to see me. What more could I have asked for in office space. I preferred small, old bars that looked as if the walls could talk. I liked jukeboxes that still played 45s, music that hadn't been rotated in forty years. I liked red leather booths and pool tables, Irish bartenders with a glimmer in their eyes and a story to tell. I liked dark bars, low-lit caves in which I could maneuver and locate a spot to observe and study. Oh, and by the way, I was the bait! I had to be. What else could I attract them with? The people I was looking for were interested in three things: Money, power, and sex. I definitely didn't have any money, and I definitely didn't have any power; it was all about sex, those three little letters that spell out such fun and opportunity. But it was just the bait. I never fully intended on using it as a way by which to finance my research. I was just interested in using it to attract information. And the easiest way to get it was to bring my subject closer, handle him intimately. The fact that they were attracted to me and usually drunk made it easier to extract the personal details of their lives, which could enrich my story and my inquisitiveness with fame. I wasn't interested in having sex with all of Hollywood, I was interested in my story and finding a job. So if having sex with one of my subjects did occur, and it did occur in Hollywood, well, then, all the more fun was involved in that evening of research.

As I mentioned earlier, I especially liked giving blow jobs. Don't ask me why, but I just liked it. Blow jobs were a way to get out of the room quicker when I was finished with my little game and the other party wasn't finished with his. So, yes, at times I used sex to get what I wanted. Cuff me.

I spent Wednesday recovering from Tuesday's hangover, staring at the Director's "thanks for the fuck" flowers and wanting to revise entirely the whole event of going out and story scoring. By Thursday morning I had revised my game plan and put to rest any ill will I was sending toward the Director. After all, Thursday night was only hours away, and I couldn't miss it if I was serious about being seen, so of course I said count me in when Carolyn called.

V.O. NARRATOR
Carolyn is my best friend. We moved to Los
Angeles together after a few too many
drinks at the Waldorf Astoria bar in New
York one rainy day in February, both of us

brokenhearted by Brat-Packers. We devised
a plan to escape New York and start our
lives over in Los Angeles. Carolyn is six
years older than me. She was from
Washington, D.C., and just out of a hairy
mess with the government that included the
shredding of a few crucial documents. She
was well educated, smart, very beautiful, a
political celebrity, and tons of fun. I could
rally her at any time to get a drink, and we
were perfect together in just about any situation. Years later, Carolyn would become a
crack addict and marry a heroin-addicted
rock and roll writer. I was in her wedding,
which is about all I can remember of that
day. Carolyn would lend me money over
the years when I was broke. I would
slowly pay her back years later.

We arranged to meet at the Olive, a low-key but "very cool, very hip" bar by the Farmer's Market on Fairfax. Thursdays at the Olive had all the right elements. It catered to a mainly "industry" crowd, so chances of running into someone I knew were good. I did the usual beautiful, understated, model makeup, just a little here and there to enhance all the right facial features and get a good glow going for an evening of low golden lights, jewel-toned fabrics and warm woods. I skipped the tight, sexy dress and pulled out the Levi's and black fisherman's turtleneck sweater so it looked like I didn't give a shit about beauty. I was confident and sexy in an East Coast sorta way. I always thought, Dress like you're in the Hamptons in Los Angeles, and dress like you're in Los Angeles in the Hamptons, and you can't miss. It never failed me on my greatest missions. The way I looked could start a conversation with the kind of man I was looking to attract, and the kind of man I was looking to attract definitely had to have lived in New York at some point. L.A. bar, I could easily be spotted. L.A. girl in New York clothes said "sexy and smart."

We sat at the bar and ordered our drinks: my usual, vodka and cranberry with lime, and her usual, chardonnay. We started working through the details of my night with the Director and what could possibly come of it. Right from the get-go, we concluded that I'd never hear from him again, much less score a part in one of his movies. But fuck that, how do I avoid the guy? He's everywhere, and besides, who the hell did he tell about our little night; now I gotta worry about all that shit as well as not having the rent to pay this month. Fuck, give me another vodka.

The furthest thing from my mind that night would have been seeing my former roommate's former lover. The last time I had seen him had been at the old love shack. We had all been playing some pajama game. Who knew what the fuck our intentions had been. I could only remember the pajamas being involved and the various faces that still haunted me on my dirt-weed high in our San Fernando Valley house. Other than that, I couldn't fill my friend Carolyn in on the facts, much less myself, when I saw him slither through the back door with some blonde chick. I felt a sudden sense of panic come over me, and the usual clammy sweat that followed a Henry sighting, and the quick eye contact that is the only cool thing to do in that situation, and then the abrupt turn back to the bartender to order yet another vodka. I wasn't sure if he caught the eye contact move, but I could surely count on my partner in crime, Carolyn, to fill me in on his upcoming moves, should any of them include coming my way. I took the much deserved "Oh fuck" moment and discussed my plan with Carolyn. Much to my dismay, Carolyn reminded me that it was not the pajama party where I had last seen him, it was the motorcycle kiss encounter when we had last seen each other. Another "Oh fuck, you're right" moment. My roommate had still been dating him when I'd given him that kiss. Well, who gives a rat's ass, I thought, she's not my roommate anymore, and that was two years ago, so fuck it. He probably doesn't even remember. Besides, I was fat then.

"Okay," I said to Carolyn, "check the fucker out and tell me what he looks like, and tell me who he's with."

Carolyn did the half bar stool turn perfectly to casually grab a snatch at him and report back to me. "Okay," she said, "he totally looks hot! And he's with some chick that's gross."

Perfect reporting. Exactly what I needed to hear. Now, I needed a plan. Simple. Wait. Wait till he comes over or close by, turn around and catch his eye.

An hour and a half went by, and still he was at the back table with the blonde chick. The longer I waited, the more boozy, sexy, disillusioned I became. After two hours, it was time for plan B: pay the check, start to leave, make eye contact with him on the turn away from the bar and score . . . sure enough, it works.

V.O. NARRATOR

I was in love with Henry the moment I saw
him, completely fascinated by the way he
walked, talked, moved, and just about
anything he could possibly do. Henry
was everything I ever wanted. He was
Canadian and a hockey player. I loved
hockey players, especially goalies, which
he was. Henry was the hockey player I
never got to flirt with, every pee-wee, Jr.
A hockey player that my brother brought
home after practice but that I could

never have. He was also dirty. So dirty
he actually smelled. I can remember my
ex showering him down before the crazy
sex they had all night long. I could hear
them through the walls, fucking and
moaning. It never turned me on. I heard
it all the time. She was always fucking
someone, but I hated that she was fucking Henry. And I hated that Henry never
noticed me. I was at my most unattrac-
tive when I met him, still waitressing in
the Valley at a pizza joint and fifteen
pounds overweight. I was broke and
didn't even want to notice myself, but I
knew Henry was the one for me. And I
thought, somehow, one day he would
see. The last time I had seen Henry he'd
paid a visit to my ex. That's when I gave
Henry a kiss. I gave him a kiss on the
lips right in front of the house. I sensed
that things were over between them and
that I would not be seeing him anytime
soon. I felt sorry for him having to come
over and say good-bye. Clearly, he was
not informed about the free love shack
business my roommate was running. So I
walked Henry out to his motorcycle and
said my good-bye as well. But I kissed
him . . . I kissed Henry . . . I kissed the
love of my life for the first time . . . He
didn't expect me to kiss him, but I did. I
kissed Henry, that's all I could say to

myself for days . . . I kissed Henry. Two
years have passed since the kiss and we
now meet again.

"Hey, baby," he said from across the room as he got up. Carolyn
and I walked over, and I gave him a big hug. I could feel all eyes
on us as we hugged, because in the two years since I had seen him,
Henry had become a huge star. Every one of his movies was grossing over 80 million dollars, his rate had gone through the roof, and
he was on his way to superstardom. But I could never really see
that part of him for some reason; I could only see this beautiful
man that I remembered so well riding up on his motorcycle all
disheveled, but glowing with light.

After the hug, which I recall as the kind where you embrace
tightly, then grab each other's hands, my life changed forever. I
knew in that moment that I had found my soul mate. Though why
him? It didn't make any sense to me. I had felt no ties to anyone
other than him in so long, and it was just a brief moment. What
the fuck was it? What had just happened to me? Why couldn't I
just carry on the same act, why didn't I want to? So many things
ran through my mind in that moment, I wasn't sure when to let go
of his hand, so I didn't. I kept holding on; clearly I had found
something to save me, someone to stop me from all the craziness I
had grown so accustomed to. I wanted to hide inside of Henry and
never let him go. I didn't care about my ego then, I didn't care
about introducing Carolyn to him, or what the blonde chick
thought, I just cared about holding on to his hand. I noticed he
wasn't letting go of my hand either. I didn't want the moment to
stop, I wanted all of time to stop, and I wanted to stay right there
with him forever. "When do I get to see you again?" spilled out of
my mouth.

We exchanged numbers, introduced our friends and said good-bye. "Oh, my God, what just happened in there?" Carolyn asked as we waited for the valet to bring around our cars. I prayed that we could get away before Henry and his friend came flying out the door. I couldn't respond with any words that could describe the way I was feeling, much less make sense of it all. I said I'd call her in the morning.

Satisfied and freaked out, we parted ways. I tried to focus on his number on the back of the matchbook, and decided I would call him the following week to invite him to my birthday party. I threw the matches next to the "thanks for the fuck" flowers on my night table and fell asleep.

OPEN BAR

Who to invite and what to wear? It was all too much. The overwhelming need to throw myself a party at such a difficult time seemed surreal, if not delusional. My ego needed tending to, and I needed an escape from the poverty and depression. Throwing myself a fabulous birthday party was the cure for both of those— or at least a temporary solution.

Driving once again over the hill from the San Fernando Valley allowed for plenty of think time and party planning fantasy on the way to my Tuesday night acting class—one of the few things I had ever committed to that involved the word *class*. I wasn't exactly a big fan of any kind of class, much less the kind with homework, but it was all part of the big plan to fulfill my destiny as a famous actress and prolong the use of my actress title. Acting class interested me for two reasons, the lesser being acting, and the primary being cheap therapy. I had been studying with the same teacher for two years, and I felt I had actually learned a few things about myself and about Chekhov. I loved the Russian playwrights. I had already become a huge supporter of their favorite import, so what the hell. I could now drink their vodka and speak fluently about their greatest playwrights, and on a good day recite monologues from *The Seagull*.

But it wasn't just the Chekhov that kept me coming back, it was the time I got to spend with Charlotte at the diner across the street after class that kept me looking forward to Tuesdays.

V.O. NARRATOR

Charlotte. The Jesus freak. The one who's always saying she'll pray for me. There were times I wished I could have given her a list of things that I was in need of. I'm sure there was a Gucci bag I had my eye on, though I suspect Charlotte's prayers were for the salvation of my soul. Charlotte spoke with a whisper of a voice, kittylike. She'd purr at you with beautiful words and promises from the Bible. Anyone would have followed in Jesus' footsteps if they had met Charlotte. Charlotte's main and most obvious features were her double D breasts, which she was convinced attracted people to Christ. "If they start a conversation about Jesus," she would say, "then I hope everyone sees them. The bigger the better." Never mind the tight blouses and form-fitting jeans that she must have painted on. It was her commitment to Jesus that made all the hooker clothes seem fine as long as she was spreading the Word. Her Bible-beater routine and the stripper with the heart of gold outfits are what attracted me to Charlotte. Somehow I knew she was going to be part of my story.

* * *

As I drove to class I thought about whether to invite Charlotte to my party. Charlotte and I had met in acting class, but as usual, I never let anyone get too close too fast. Seeing Charlotte once a week seemed like enough for me, and she sure as hell wasn't my type of girlfriend, much less someone I would have become friends with outside of class, so really, I just considered us acquaintances. Then one night after class she came over to me and asked me if I'd like to join her for coffee at the diner next door. I believe the answer no was on my mind, but the word yes came out of my mouth. Old manners haunt sometimes. With a Marlboro Lite in hand, I followed Charlotte into the diner and quickly grabbed the darkest booth I could find. The thought of coffee so late in the evening irked me, so I ordered a Coke and fries with ranch dressing. I just listened and watched Charlotte speak. Instantly, I noticed she had a calming effect on me. Her presence was comforting. I didn't know how she did it.

Meeting at the diner became a weekly ritual, though I hardly spoke to Charlotte the first few months. I was usually too tired, too hungover from the night before, or any number of reasons I couldn't give her the time of day, yet I still agreed to join her at the diner every Tuesday night. I'd tell her I was too tired to talk, and she'd continue to sip her decaf and watch me light Marlboros and eat my fries. Then, one night after class I waited for her to meet me behind the theater so we could walk to the diner together, and she didn't show. When I returned home there was a message on my machine.

CHARLOTTE
Hi Tobi, it's Charlotte. I'm sorry that I
didn't wait for you after class tonight but
I think for now it's just better we see each
other in class. I don't think it's the right

> time in your life to start a new friendship
> with all that you have going on. Know
> that I'm always there for you if you need
> me. . . . Okay then, take care. I'll see you
> in class on Tuesday.

I lost a friend because I couldn't give—what the fuck was that all about? I give all fuckin' day long. What do you mean I can't give? And what the hell am I supposed to give, goddamn it! I slammed down the phone and fell onto my bed crying. I thought to myself, how can I give? What do I do to give? I've never had to give, I always take. . . . I don't know how to give. I wanted nothing more in that moment than to close my eyes and sleep. I hated the pain that Charlotte was causing me, I hated having to face who I had become. I knew what Charlotte wanted from me. She wanted me to listen. She wanted me to believe what she had to say about salvation and God's plan for forgiveness and repentance and holiness and prayer and worship and praise and all the other words I had never heard before. She wanted me to understand that there was a way out of my life, that I could walk away and begin anew. She couldn't take me there, she could only guide me and share with me how it was on the other side, because she knew I was still living in my favorite place of darkness and all the time we had spent at the diner were my only moments of light, but that too had to come to an end. I would now have to find the light on my own. Charlotte had done all she could. By showing me the road. It was up to me to walk down it.

V.O. NARRATOR
> I don't know how we choose the right
> path. God puts these people into our lives
> every moment of every day, trying to

guide us through this world and we're
supposed to notice them. We can either
see the message he is sending or we can
just walk on by. Like passing a homeless
person who's begging for money. Do you
give or don't you? You have to decide
right then and there. It's no different
when angels cross your path, pointing out
the right turn. You can't trust yourself to
believe angels exist. You have to know
what faith means. But I didn't know how
to get it. Who gives faith? Where the hell
do you get faith? Is it in all those unseen
things? What was Charlotte trying to say
to me that I couldn't understand? How
could she have faith that everything
would work out okay? I couldn't choose
her path. I didn't have faith. I'd have to
learn what faith meant on my own. I'd
have to walk in my own footsteps.

I was back on the fast track and had found my stride. Charlotte
was only a buzz kill now, so whether to invite her to my fabulous
party confused me. I wanted her there to see why I was so fucked
up, but I also didn't want her to know. Partly because I knew she'd
never been to such a groovy event, and partly because I thought
she was the one who could save me should anything go wrong. I
wanted her to be the designated friend. Yet I didn't want her to
keep me from the sinners either. So I found a way, as usual, to
invite her and make it work for me as well. I told her she could
come, but she had to come alone. That way for sure, I thought, she
wouldn't show, and if she did, so what, so she sees how hideous

I've become, who gives a fuck anyway, it's my birthday. But I knew that I was falling and I knew that I wanted Charlotte there to catch me. And I knew that she was the only one who could. Still, if I could just show her how different my life was compared to hers, maybe she'd understand why I drank, why I smoked, why I fucked men I didn't love, and why I hated myself so much. I rolled into class and sat in the back row, weighing my options before speaking to Charlotte. Before I even said hello, I asked her. As her eyes lit up to be polite and say yes, she said no. "I'm sorry, I just can't, but thank you for thinking of me." I told her where and what time in case she changed her mind. I dropped my head down to my chest and walked outside. I felt empty inside, but the need to find my story gave me legs to keep walking. "Don't look back," I thought to myself. "Never look back. Just go home. Just drive . . ."

An immediate need to put my emotions in place and silence the pain was what usually set off the cleaning fits. Although my apartment above the garage was just one room with a small bathroom, stall shower and a kitchenette, I could spend hours cleaning it. It never mattered what time of day I began cleaning, it only mattered that I finish the job completely. I found that this was the only thing I could do to stave off the feeling of rejection from Charlotte. Cleaning was a mission in which I could focus on the details and solve the problem. See that the floor was dirty, sweep it; fill the bathroom sink with Spic and Span, then mop it, done. See that the shower had soap scum on the walls; spray it with Tilex then sponge it off. With each segment of the room I cleaned I sensed accomplishment and reward. There was now placement and order for all the disorder around me. I could control the environment completely. There were no booby traps, no rejections, no crowds. I was safe. I could have a panic attack if I wanted, I was home; I could experience all the things that would happen to me on the outside, yet feel completely safe in my own environment, and I could continue to clean until the pain would vacate. I could tire myself scrubbing floors, washing dishes, arranging glasses, cleaning makeup drawers, changing sheets, rehanging clothes, until I could no longer stand, until I could only wash my hands of all the dust and dirt and fall into bed, where finally I could rest and all my madness could cover me. I had completed something. I was in control. Things were in order for tomorrow and I needed things to be in order, for tomorrow was the day I had to make all the birthday party calls and put the finishing touches on the plans for my party. I had cleaned the weakness away. I could once again awake to walk over whomever I needed to make my plans happen. I could lie to get what I wanted and I could pretend to be whoever I wanted to be and with whomever I chose. I fell asleep with things in order the way I needed them to be, the way I arranged them to be. It was my order, it was my house. Never mind the memories of Mom and Dad fighting, never mind hiding in the basement crouched under the staircase, my bare feet cold on the cement floor. I can't go there now. I have to sleep. I've cleaned. I've put those memories away.

I take a deep breath, put my hands over my face and push the hot air through the cracks in my fingertips and run away from it all: The sounds of my father's raging voice and my mother's exhausted pleas to him to stop. I pull my knees to my stomach and curl up, waiting for the silence to catch me so I can close my eyes and pretend to sleep. I hear my mother's voice echo in the darkness. Quietly, she makes her way down the hallway to speak through the crack in the door of my bedroom: "There's always tomorrow to make your dreams come true."

My first thoughts upon waking were puppies, a joint and an Egg McMuffin. I had puppy madness. A desperate desire to own one even though I couldn't begin to support one, much less care for one. Still I wanted one badly, which just meant I was lonely and in need of affection, generally the way I felt after the big clean-up.

I rolled my home-grown, a pre-birthday gift courtesy of friend Fun Boy, and kicked it a little until an outfit came to mind. Then, bingo, with a light buzz on, I had all the answers. I had an outfit, a plan, places to go, things to do, food to get, and calls to make. I was temporarily cured. The curse was lifted. The phone rang.

"This is Sweet Lady Jane calling to confirm your birthday cake order for the three-berry cake for fifty."

"Great," I answered. "I'll pick it up on Saturday." I hung up the phone. Oh shit, I thought to myself, the fuckin' party. What am I going to wear to the party? Shit . . . my sunny buzz was gone.

I needed to make the birthday calls, particularly the one to Henry. Henry was the most important call. Without Henry my party would be a disaster. I would have no one to go home with. The party was just the excuse to see Henry again. I needed a reason to call, and I couldn't just call and say hi. So fuck it, now the party was about Henry and nothing else. Everything—from the details to where and what time it would be—only bored me unless I thought of having Henry there.

My first call was to secure free drinks at a club. I needed to guarantee the manager there would be famous faces and loads of models. I went over my guest list slowly, so as to sound unrehearsed and casual about my connections. I figured the best way to start was to throw out a few local clubgoers, then move into Young Hollywood, toss in some old-timers, and round off the list with "Bobby and some of his friends may show up. And Sean is definitely coming." Any club owner worth two cents knows that's Robert De Niro and Sean Penn. And if you have to ask you're an idiot!

"I got these people coming. So-and-so may show, but who

knows, she's definitely coming, and yes I called Ford, they know. Jack, who knows, maybe he'll come after the game." That's how it went. BA DA BING . . . Free drinks till one o'clock, and the fucker said he'd pick up the tab for the cake as well. With that, I was warmed up and ready to invite my guests. That was easy. A quick and casual call. I was calling during the day, it was all machine work. "Hey, it's Tobs, I'm having a little get-together (I always made everything seem small, so as not to scare the natives), Saturday night at Bar One, eight o'clock, bring someone if you want and I'll see ya there, okay, hope all's well, take care." And that was it. I made all fifty calls, except the one to Henry. I was saving his for last. I wanted to call him in the evening. I wanted to talk to him in person.

I pulled out the matches with his phone number and dialed. His machine picked up immediately.

"Hey, it's Henry, leave a message. . . ."

"Hey, Henry, it's Tobi. It was good to see you the other night. Listen, I'm having a little get-together for my birthday Saturday night, and if you're in town I'd love it if you could drop by. I'll leave your name at the Door. It's at Bar One, eight o'clock, okay, so I hope to see you there, take care."

I hung up the phone and let out a sigh. Great, now I don't know for sure if he's coming or not, I don't know if he's in town or not, I don't know shit. Okay, whatever, I thought, I just gotta move forward, and if he shows he shows, and if he doesn't he doesn't. What now, I thought, what do I need in this moment? A drink. And possibly another ceremonial joint to smooth out the rough edges. So with plan intact, I ran out the door, no makeup, jeans, cowboy boots, black leather blazer, a healthy attitude and a couple of twenty spots Western Unioned to me earlier by Mom as a sorta pre-birthday gift to pay the electric bill. I was good for a couple of vodkas and then I was out. I figured I had driven "over the hill" about a thousand times that day, and the last trip back might actually make me want to drive right off the side of Laurel Canyon once I hit Mulholland. I thought of James Dean in his convertible and that Billy Joel song "Only the Good Die Young" and my mom's haunting voice speaking through my door at night.

The phone rings, it's too early too face the blinding California light that pierces my bamboo shades. I hesitate but answer it with my muffled morning sexy booze voice.

KANE
"Tobi, hey, it's Kane"

Though Kane is my brother, we barely know each other. The once scrawny kid that beat and humiliated me is now 6'4" and about 210 pounds. His nickname is "Chief." Hearing his voice on the other end of the phone startles me, as I am reminded of the phone call we had before my parents split up for the last time. "They're splitting up again, do what you can to get out of here before it gets any worse." Kane; always the realist, just stating the facts. Without emotion, without reaction. "I'm going to Des Moines to play Junior A with the Buckaneers." It had been easy for Kane to just leave. He'd already had a plan and somewhere to go. He'd just said, "That's it for you and me, kid. The fake family show is over, you're on your own." But there hadn't been any time for our feelings to show. Both of us had needed to get out of the house, get away from all the yelling and screaming. Kane's ticket had just happened to come before mine.

We have nothing in common now. His constant name calling and beatings when I was younger sour thoughts of him as an adult. He married my best friend Willow from junior high. I introduced them when she spent a night after cheerleading camp. They ended up making out in Kane's room to *Frampton Comes Alive*. They later had two kids and moved to Dallas. True love. The perfect life. They hate me. "Willow and I are thinking of coming out to celebrate your birthday. How does that sound?" Willow serves cocktails on flights across America and gets free tickets galore for the two of them to travel anywhere on standby.

Without a pause, I hear the word "great" come flying from my mouth. A knee-jerk reaction to hearing my brother's voice. Too hungover to come up with a lie.

Ten minutes later it was settled. They were coming, and they were staying with me. Their plane would be arriving late, so they would have to meet me at the party. Well, I thought to myself, that sounds dangerous, but what the hell. They're big kids now. I was fighting a surreal headache and about to head into the bathroom when another call clicked in. I quickly said good-bye to my brother and answered the call.

HENRY
Hey, Tobs, it's Henry. So, it's your birthday.

TOBI
Yeah, so are you going to be in town?

HENRY
Well, I'm not sure, but if I am, I'll be there.

Typical bullshit actor answer, I thought to myself; however, I was cautious not to let my tone of voice show my disdain for the casual response. It was time for the confident comeback.

TOBI
Oh, yeah, totally. If you're in town, then

come on by. If not, we'll hook up another
time.

HENRY
Okay, cool.

We quickly bullshitted. "How are you," "what's up with you," "how's acting going," "have you seen so-and-so." That was it. As quick as the call came, it went. What a morning. Completely forgetting my brother's call, I focused on the few words I had spoken to Henry. *Shit,* I thought, *what did I say? Did I sound too casual or fucked up? I didn't know. *Fuck, I hate this self-deprecating crap.* Why couldn't I just hang up the phone and move on? Why did I have to relive each moment as if some Olympic judge were watching? *Whatever, I did my best, for Christ's sake. I was hungover.* And then I remembered his voice, his sexy, beautiful voice: "Hey, it's Henry." And I heard him saying it over and over again till I rolled out of bed and rushed to the toilet. I never paid much attention to throwing up, it was par for the course, part of the price I paid for my party girl status, but I hated the look on my face as I came up to the mirror. "Who are you?" I'd point and ask the mirror, "Who are you?"

INT. BAR ONE NIGHTCLUB, SUNSET STRIP
Low-lit, badly decorated, even for a '90s nightclub. Wrap-
around bar separating the restaurant from the dance floor. A
pool table in the center of the club surrounded by plush couches
and coffee tables.

RESTAURANT MANAGER
Listen, I said sixty is all I can comp and
that's it. I gotta stick to what we agreed
upon, it's gonna be busy tonight.

TOBI

Yeah, but hey! We agreed it was open bar
till one o'clock, not fuckin' ten o'clock. My
friends don't even get out of bed till ten, so
can we work something out here?

RESTAURANT MANAGER

Tobs, listen, twelve o'clock is the best I can
do. And only sixty comps, you got it?

TOBI

Yeah, I got it.

Dealing with management wasn't my favorite way to start my
party, but a deal had to be struck. That settled, I was on to more
important things, like my hair. Of course, I'd had it done for the
evening, something that really wasn't my style, being the self-taught
genius I thought I was with hair and makeup. But I wasn't one to
turn down a freebie from a well-known stylist, who'd offered it as
a kind of birthday gift. So with very little maintenance ahead of me
for the night, I could ensure a good liquoring up. Champagne was
my drink of choice. What else would a birthday girl drink? I loved
champagne. What a great high, all giggly and lovable. Just enough
to have fun and keep an eye on the door for Henry's entrance. The
few bugs I had up my ass about my brother and his wife flying in,
and the possibility of Charlotte showing up, were slowly leaving my
brain, chased away by champagne bubbles.

I arrived solo. Knowing there was a way to escape or make a get-
away at a moment's notice made life easier. I wanted to leave with
Henry, if he showed, and coming alone could guarantee me that
much. I stuck it out in the club early with no one there. Dressed and
ready for my guests to arrive, I checked the list, chatted with the

bartenders, joked with the cocktail waitresses, rearranged chairs, consulted with the DJ, made countless trips to the rest room to wipe my sweaty pits with toilet paper and blot my lipstick, returned to the bar on each lap around the club to pick up a fresh glass of free bubbly and check the list. Finally they began to arrive. One by one, they came with kisses and presents, and little stories and big hugs. I was taken to the bar for drink after drink. No sign of Henry or my brother. Three sheets to the wind, most of my guests having arrived, I didn't care if my brother's plane was late or crashed. I left his name at the door and wished him the best. But it was getting late and still no Henry. I felt a tinge of sadness as I realized my new age and saw the large inferno coming toward me and the sound of "Happy Birthday." I drew in a deep breath and glanced at the crowd that had gathered around me. There he was, standing at the back of the club. I said a small thank you to the heavens and blew out the candles.

Standing in the dim red light, Henry was the most beautiful man I had ever seen. He was uncomfortable, dirty, graceful and clumsy all at the same time. A reluctant star, he slipped shyly to the back booth and hunched over a pint glass. His shiny Hawaiian black hair and his pale white skin set him apart. His brown almond-shaped eyes pierced me. A shock of bangs hung in his face to cover and comfort his soul. He radiated a sweetness I couldn't explain, the shyness of a boy in a man's body. His feet grounded on the earth, centered like a ballet dancer with his straight spine being pulled to the sky, a sense of entitlement, with hands that could carry a baby through a burning building. Every inch of his body oozed dirty, beautiful sex. That was Henry viewed from afar. That was the Henry I had to have, if only for a night, if only for a few moments.

I was through chatting with my guests. It was time to grab Henry and go. I just needed to find my brother and his wife to give them the keys to my apartment. Suddenly, I felt someone grab my arm. I turned around on a half point toe move and found myself face-to-face with Charlotte. It was like running into Jesus. Busted. Drunk and high on a little weed I had managed to get my hands on in the ladies' room, I was at a loss for words and running out of time to get to Henry. Charlotte represented the crossroad; I had to choose. I could have Charlotte drive me home and comfort me with her presence or push her completely out of my way. I could choose to walk down a new road in the morning, free of all the bullshit and start my new year clean, sober and safe, or hit the road with Jack Kerouac. In an instant, I waved Charlotte off with a smile, an excuse and a laugh and headed toward Henry. What was a friend worth, anyway, unless they had something to offer me. It hadn't lasted in the past and there was no proof of it lasting in the future, so I walked toward the moments I could create immediately. I could hide in Henry, I could pretend with Henry, and I didn't have to face reality. Charlotte had hurt me. She had stopped seeing me, stopped teaching me, stopped listening to me, and I couldn't find what she was telling me to find on my own. I yearned for the darkness and the depression I had become accustomed to. I thrived on it. It was Henry now that I had to share that with. Henry would understand how I needed to hide in him.

The plan was simple. Find Henry and suggest we leave. The fewer words the better. Henry was a simple man, and the more body language he could read, the better. Words only complicated matters. He wanted life to be simple, beautiful and natural. So, organically drunk, I suggested we leave and go to his hotel room since my brother and his wife were shacking up in my pad. We were clear on what we wanted. A safe place, a small dark room, clean sheets, holding each other.

Henry's room at the Chateau Marmont was home to him. There were books stacked on the table, piles of scripts and small pieces of torn paper with phone numbers on them. I noticed the day-old baskets of flowers sent over from the agents, producers, directors. I smelled leftover pizza and counted the empty bottles of beer on the floor: ten. The bed and bathroom were freshly cleaned. I worried about what to wear to bed. Would we even end up in bed? Henry moved with confidence in his room, unlike the shy boy at the party. He was in his castle now. We could have stayed friends that night, we didn't have to become lovers, we could never have kissed. But we did. And we kissed all night long, all over our naked bodies. Every inch of our souls went into the discovery of all the humanness we had to offer. We abstained from making love and were satisfied with how far we had gone. We knew we had time, years if we wanted. There was no hurry, only hunger. We were separated from the world.

I fell in love with Henry that night, and from that moment on there would be no one else who could make me feel the way that he did. No one else that could hold me as he did or kiss me like he did. I wanted only Henry now and whatever it would take to keep him. I wanted the moments of peace that he brought that night to last forever. But, as the sun broke the darkness, I knew I'd have to return home without him and face my own hellish reality. I left Henry in bed after a breakfast of eggs Benedict and fresh juice. We kissed good-bye at the door, and Henry slumped back into bed. I missed him as soon as I walked out of the room. I walked out of the hotel barefoot, in a borrowed T-shirt and a pair of Henry's old jeans, toward Sunset, carrying my heels in one hand and my party dress in the other. I hailed a cab and within five minutes located my lonely vehicle.

I was apprehensive about my next mission. Where had Kane and Willow ended up? From what little I could remember of the night before, I had taken my house key off my chain and handed it to him with my address scribbled on a cocktail napkin and a few lame directions. I figured I had done my part in welcoming them to Los Angeles by giving them a cool pad to stay at and a bitchin' party to attend. All the same, I feared the worst. The truth was I hadn't really taken care of them as I should have, and I was not in any state to face Kane's lashings. I wondered as I drove home what to say, what gesture to make to smooth things over. I thought of restaurants to take them to for breakfast as I thought of Henry back in his room. I hadn't let go of him yet. I could still smell him and feel his hands touching my lips and face. I wanted to stay in dreamland, but the complicated details of my morning sobered the thoughts of Henry that were making me wet all over again.

I was always uncomfortable with family visiting me in L.A. I didn't want them to expose me. Let the cat out of the bag I was just a simple girl from Michigan. I feared they could possibly blow my cover on my new and invented Hollywood starlet game. Maybe even post flyers of me as a brunette. They reminded me of the blank state that I had come from. I was anxious about the rumors that could start from them observing a day in my life. I felt ashamed that I had not met their expectations of me. I never finished high school, I never went to Michigan State, I didn't own a home. I didn't have a steady job, and I wasn't, as far as they knew, in any kind of relationship that was going anywhere, least of all marriage. Anything you were supposed to do by the time you were twenty-four and from Michigan, I didn't do. By their Midwestern standards, I was failing. I wanted nothing to do with any of the emotions that lay ahead of me, and yet I wanted them to recognize the pain I was in. Would my brother see the signs? Had he noticed my behavior? Had I said anything to offend him or his wife? What were the repairs I had to face inside my own house, inside my own heart? I didn't want to have to tell them. I just wanted them to see it for themselves and to relieve me of the burden of having to speak it. I couldn't speak it. I just wanted them to understand.

I noticed the rent-a-car in the driveway. *Fuck, they're here!* I put the car in park and jammed my too-tight heels onto my swollen feet. I decided to start with an apology and a giggle and hoped they'd be in a good mood. As I approached, the Dutch door was half-open. Their packed bags were visible.

KANE

We're gonna get going. We've been waiting
for you to call all morning and we're hungry
and tired. We've got friends down in San
Diego we can visit, and some in Manhattan
Beach, so we've decided to leave you alone
here and catch up with you some other time.

Willow said nothing as I dropped my shit on the floor and sank into my only chair. Soon they were out and headed down south. We did the kiss and good-bye thing, the thanks for last night thing, and they pointed to my gift on the floor, which they had lugged all the way from home. I didn't follow them out. I didn't help them with their luggage. I didn't care. I didn't have it in me to care for a family I was trying to forget. I had traded them in for the bigger and better deal, and they knew it. It wasn't something I wanted to have happen. Part of me wished they would have grabbed my arm and shaken me until I'd confessed my plan to live the way I had been living. I wished they'd sat me down and told me they loved me before hauling me off to some detox resort. But they just walked out, disappointed. I just sat in my lawn chair. I had better things to think about. I had Henry.

I waved good-bye from the bay window and felt numb. I wasn't driving anymore. I wasn't steering my own life. There wasn't a plan. It was about surviving from one day to the next. Climbing the walls in front of me one at a time. Gathering funds to support the behavior and buying time to further the chances of getting the story. The story was all that mattered. And now Henry.

WEDNESDAY NIGHT

Running a Door wasn't something I chose to do, it was something I ended up doing, the last stop on a long journey of hunting for the perfect job. Cash was king and I needed a job that was speaking the same language. There wasn't time for waiting on checks or getting paid two weeks after starting. It was about having the cash in hand after the job was done.

I wanted to work at night. I wanted to work by myself, I wanted to have a drink when I wanted a drink. I wanted to be able to make a few phone calls when I wanted to shoot the shit with my friends, and I needed some action to look at. I thought about being a bartender in a really cool bar or a hostess at some hot restaurant, but never did I give a thought to running a Door. I was just looking for a job when the phone rang.

                              TOBI
          Hello.

                            STEVEN
          Tobs?

TOBI
Yeah.

STEVEN
It's Steven.

TOBI
Who?

STEVEN
Steven, from New York.

TOBI
Oh, Steven, oh yeah. Sorry, man, it's been such a shitty day and I've had all these hideous phone calls from one asshole to the next, so what's up? How's the bar coming along?

STEVEN
Well, actually, I have a proposition for you.

TOBI
Oh yeah, what's that?

STEVEN
I need someone to run the Door.

TOBI
Oh, so you're looking for someone to run the Door, huh?

STEVEN

Yeah. I thought you might be interested.

TOBI

Me? You're asking me to do it?

STEVEN

Yeah, well you said you were looking for
work?

TOBI

Yeah, well, no, I mean yeah, but I've never
run a Door.

STEVEN

I know, but you know everybody, and
that's all it takes. Besides, I'll teach you.

TOBI

What do you mean?

STEVEN

I'll stand behind the Door and teach you,
that's what I mean. So what do you think?

TOBI

I don't know, Steven. I mean, yeah, I know
everybody, but I've never done it.

STEVEN

Just try it, okay? I think you'd be perfect.

TOBI

Yeah, okay. When do you want me to start?

STEVEN

Tonight.

TOBI

Tonight? You want me to start tonight?

STEVEN

Yeah, it's Wednesday. It will be slow, so
you can be ready for Friday.

TOBI

Okay, what the fuck. How much do I get
paid?

STEVEN

A hundred bucks a night, cash; then when
things pick up, a hundred and fifty bucks a
night. Deal?

TOBI

Okay, deal.

STEVEN

Be at the bar at seven and I'll introduce you
to some of the guys. I'm pretty sure Billy and
Daniel will be on the Door with you. I'll
have two guys outside and three inside,
plus head of security on walkie-talkie, and
oh, yeah, I'll be right behind the door with

you all the way. Okay? I'll see you at seven
o'clock. Dress warm and in black except a
colored shirt. Oh, yeah, Tobs? I think
you're gonna like it. Something just tells
me you're gonna like it. . . .

Seven o'clock would come all too quickly. It was early October
and the nights were getting chilly. I was worried about staying
warm. I rumbled through my clothes, trying to find the perfect
look. I pulled out all my old jackets from New York and laid them
on the bed. I wanted something that showed power. I wanted to
stay warm but look cool as well. I tried on the black leather blazer I usually wore with jeans, motorcycle boots and a blue dress
shirt. I looked in the mirror and hated it. I tried black jeans, a
black turtleneck under a white dress shirt, black boots and my
black aviator jacket. I tore it off and threw it in the reject pile on
the floor.

Now it was six o'clock and it was starting to get dark. I was
convinced that I had nothing to wear and that I was just gonna call
Steven and tell him to forget it. I was tired of the dressing game,
and for what? What was this job all about anyway? It was already
stressing me out, and the thought of standing outside on the street
all night seemed lonely and scary, but then my long black overcoat
on the bed caught my eye. I hadn't worn it since I'd left New York,
and something about it just seemed like it was worth one more try
in the ol' dressing department. I put on my long silk underwear,
then my heavy ski socks. I searched my closet for my black leather
jeans and threw them on. I grabbed my red turtleneck and pulled
it over my long underwear top. I looked in the mirror. So far, so
good. I needed more. The white shirt again, I thought, checking my
watch from moment to moment; I was running out of time. I threw
on the white dress shirt over the red turtleneck and tucked it into

my leather pants, pulled on my motorcycle boots and picked up my black wool overcoat and put it on. I looked in the mirror. Something was missing. I needed a hat. There was no time to try on fuckin' hats. Thinking fast, I grabbed my baseball hat with an American flag on it. *Done. Okay, that's it, I'm ready. One more time. Do I need anything? Yes, shit! Gloves. Where are my fuckin' gloves? Don't panic. Look with the ski stuff. Shit, where's the fuckin' ski stuff?*

Suddenly everything came to a screeching halt. I felt a jolt in my heart. It was like watching a car accident. This one was quick and fast. It stole the air from my lungs and sent me bending over my bed and grabbing the iron rails just to brace myself. *No, not tonight, not tonight, just let me breathe, just let me sit here on the bed and stop for a few seconds and then I'll be fine.*

I sat on the edge of my bed, holding the rail with one hand and bracing my chest with the other. I sat quietly, listening for my heartbeats to get in sync. I counted the pulse beats on my neck with two fingers and waited. I breathed in through my nose and out through my mouth like the cardiologists had instructed. *Please, God, please. Not now, please just this once, I've been doing so good, just let me breathe.* Finally, after about five minutes, it was over. I was sweating from all the layers of clothes and the scare of the panic attack. But I couldn't stop this time, I couldn't give in, I had to get up off the bed, I had to make it to work or I'd lose my only chance at making some money and staying in L.A. I looked at my watch. It was 6:15. How could so much have happened in just fifteen minutes? Relieved that I still had time to make it to the club without being late, I pulled myself from the bed and walked into the bathroom to wipe the sweat from my face and check my make-up again. I opened the medicine cabinet, grabbed two extra-strength Motrin, pulled my hair into a ponytail, tossed my hat on again, and headed out the door.

The drive from Studio City was my favorite part of the commute into Los Angeles. I usually took Laurel Canyon over the hill if I was gonna be on the east side of town. I loved the way Laurel Canyon wound down into the city toward the center of town. The drive over the hill gave me a chance to reflect on the events that had just occurred and gave me a chance to feel as though I was leaving one world and entering another. Each time I saw the lights emerge on Sunset Boulevard as I approached the city, I felt a key turn inside of me. Open for business, open for new ideas, ready to try anything.

I headed down La Brea and took a left on Melrose toward the club. I had fifteen minutes left. Fifteen minutes until my life would change forever. I parked my car across from the club and turned off the engine. I cracked my window, lit a cigarette, and watched the Front Door. This is it, I thought. I looked again in the rearview mirror and caught the very top of my baseball hat. I tipped the hat up and saw my green eyes looking deep into my own soul. "This is it, hon," I said to myself. "This is what it's gonna take with you, ain't it? You're just gonna have to do things the hard way, aren't you?"

I looked away from the mirror, locked up the car and walked across the street toward the Door. My Door. I opened it and walked in.

Lights behind the bar and a few lanterns on the wall illuminated the space. The walls were dark oak, and the carpet was a deep red. It didn't seem at all like the place I had seen during construction. It was dark, gloomy, a vacuum of isolated time. It seemed to suck me in and pull me toward the bar. The ceilings, however high, became low and comforting; it was a box, a safe little box to hide in. The sound of the air conditioner blowing and the waitresses complaining about the cold comforted me, as their high-pitched whinny noises were muffled with each new push of air through the vents. I focused on each and every one of them as I watched them grab and count their trays, fold napkins and clean the menus. I watched as they chatted and laughed and noticed how, without a hitch, they seemed to do each and every task without looking up once to acknowledge the other, their busy hands never stopping until a pile of napkins or menus had been completed. And then I remembered the gloves. I had forgotten the gloves at home. Shit, I thought. I knew I'd forget something.

I sat patiently at the bar. I could see the back of the bartender's head at the other end of the bar; I wasn't sure that he could see me, but then he turned around.

JONNIE
Oh my fucking God, it's you.

TOBI
Jonnie, is that you?

JONNIE
Yeah, it's me, what the fuck are you doing here?

TOBI
What am I doing here—what are you doing here?

JONNIE
I work here.

TOBI
Oh yeah, well I work here too.

JONNIE
No fuckin' way. You're it, you're the Door
person?

TOBI
Yep, sure as shit am, Jonnie.

JONNIE
Holy shit, well let's drink to that. Let's
drink to that.

We split a Coke, clicked our glasses and smiled. I had known Jonnie for years from various clubs in Los Angeles, and he had always been nice to me. I was glad that he was here. It just all started to seem so right. Jonnie was gonna be the bartender. Steven owned the club, all my friends knew I would be working there and told me they were gonna come by and see me, I mean, what could be more perfect, I thought. I was happy. I had finally found something that felt right, and more important, somewhere I could find my story. Jonnie told me that Steven was upstairs and just to wait for him to come down. The club had already been open for two months before I had heard from Steven, and I knew there was gonna be some hell to pay from the guys I was gonna be working with, but I didn't know what had gone down with the Door guy before me, so I just thought I wouldn't ask unless they brought it up.

I saw Steven coming down the stairs with the clipboard, the walkie-talkies, the clickers, the guest list and two very large guys dressed in black. I put out my cigarette and sat up straight.

STEVEN
Tobs, this is Billy and Daniel, they're
working outside with you tonight. This is

your guest list, your walkie-talkies, and two clickers. Billy and Daniel are gonna take care of you tonight, so if there's anything you need, just let them know and they'll take care of it. So, any questions? Don't worry, I'm gonna be right there behind the Door. Okay, kids, let's rock and roll.

Billy was black Irish from the south shore of Boston, who had ranked in Golden Gloves, played Junior A hockey, and loved watching any sport on television. He had a smile a mile wide and a story to go with it. A real man's man, he preferred the kind of conversation that happens in locker rooms, as opposed to the long-winded Sturm und Drang of everyday life. He had moved to Los Angeles looking for work as an actor after New York had given him the once-over in the theater district. Billy had been working Doors for six years when I met him. He was one of the best. He knew everybody and everybody liked him. Most importantly, he could fight. Billy worked the Front Door. He hated Inside. He liked it outside in the cold. The colder the better for Billy. He was always hot. Just a black leather blazer and T-shirt in the middle of winter. He was always slapping his fists together, saying, "What's it gonna be tonight, kids, what's it gonna be?"

Daniel was Billy's best friend. Daniel stood 6'2" and weighed roughly 185 pounds. He was strong, yet he had the heart of a kitten. A German heritage and a blonde head of hair to match gave Daniel the perfect combination of intimidation and strength. Daniel was the good cop to Billy's bad cop. Daniel was new to the Door, he had only gotten the gig because of Billy. He had never worked outside before and never at the Front Door. Billy, however, had wanted someone he liked to help the night pass by quicker, and Daniel had been the answer. So Daniel was in, just like that. All it had taken was for Billy to get him the introduction to Steven, and the next night he was at the Front Door. Billy and Daniel were inseparable after work as well. They ran together, played hockey on the same team, and chased women all over town. Daniel would one day die of heat exhaustion in Billy's arms in the Hollywood Hills.

For the most part, the first few hours were quiet. There was a little action at the Door, mostly dinner reservations. I listened as Billy and Daniel talked about the Rangers game on TV. I watched as they used their hands, gesticulating with every word. It seemed like a dance to me—they spoke on and on about each play, meticulously describing each player, each goal, each check. As they continued their stories, I could hear nothing but the sound of their black leather gloves slapping together as one would burst out in excitement, describing the game and punching his fist into the glove. I heard only this because I was watching and waiting. Watching the streets, watching each car pull up in front of the valet, watching each person get out, making mental notes, what kind of car they drove, who they were arriving with, what time they were arriving, were they coming for dinner or drinks, and who they were. That was the most important thing about the Door. Never forget a face. And never the name that matched that face. I remained quiet and greeted each guest, checked my list, motioned for Billy or Daniel to open the Door, and waited. I waited for ten o'clock. That was when the real show was about to begin. Everything up until then was just dress rehearsal.

Up until this point I had not turned anyone away from the Door. Every person who had come to the Door had had a reservation for dinner or was on the list. I knew that Billy and Daniel were waiting for me to start turning people away, but until now there had been no reasons to do so. I knew that I had to be quick with my decisions, look the person straight in the eye, turn them away and stick to the choice I had made; however, I had never done it before, especially with Billy and Daniel watching and Steven behind the Door.

I knew the basic rules, and I figured if I just stuck to them I could at least get by for the night. No groups of guys early in the night, or ever. Pack the club with beautiful women early in the evening. Get all the reservations in without asking any names on the list. Check the clickers for the count before eleven o'clock. No Persians, no Arabs, no hookers, no kids under the age of twenty-one unless they're actors. Look for guns. No drunks, save space for after midnight, watch the street for limos and town cars, call in checks on the walkies every fifteen minutes, watch out for the cop cars on the street, look for the fire marshall at all times, and just say no. . . and keep saying no until you mean it. And never second-guess your decision, even if you were wrong. 'Cause that's the only way you'll make it. That's the only way. . . .

V.O. NARRATOR

I thought about getting out the very first night
I started. It was like a dangerous drug, saying
no and having so much power to determine
the outcome of one person's fate. Each time I
turned someone away at the Door, I could feel
the gratification of actually believing my own
lie. The power to say no was an addiction.
Every time I successfully turned someone
away at the Door it made it easier for the next
time and then the next. Saying no was like
shooting the main line and having confidence
all at the same time, and it was free. It was
the perfect cocktail for my low self-esteem.

Yes, I had discovered my Utopia, my new and
most powerful drug. That was it, that's all it
took for me to get hooked, just one little
word with two letters in it. That's right, sign
me up! 'Cause I wanted more after that very
first "no" I spoke right there on Melrose
Avenue to a little, short, fifty-year-old man
dangling a gold Rolex watch in my face,
offering it to me if I would let him in. I mean,
I really didn't expect it to feel quite that good,
but it was like a fix. And for those six to eight
hours at the Door, I was in control. Not my
landlord to whom I owed money, or the bank
that owned my car, or the agents who
wouldn't take a meeting with me to help my
acting career, none of those people were in
charge of me or my life at the Door. It was
just me. It was a relief to go to work and
leave my uncertain world to stand outside a
fuckin' Door and control things for a while.
That was the juice I pumped myself up with
night after night, just waiting to leave my real
world and enter into the one in which I could
create and re-create each and every night,
depending upon how much I needed to get
the rush.

My first night at the Door was over. Dexter was head of security; he
called for the last count and called the check-in on the walkie-talkies
to check and lock all exits. Like a lion, I stood at the Door, a statue
as I said my good nights, gave my kisses, remembered the faces,
watched which couples hooked up and left together, remembered

what cars they got into, and then bid adieu to the last lonely actor/director/waiter. And locked my Front Door and took my first breath of the evening, stared right down the bar into Steven's eyes, looked at my clipboard, now all scratched out with circled names, crossed my hands in front of my long, heavy, black overcoat and dropped my head down with shame. When I lifted my eyes to focus back on Steven, he was gone. Every step that I took toward the bar to order a drink from Jonnie lasted a lifetime in my memory. Each step, I noticed something different about me, something heavier. My shoulders were more pronounced, my stride longer, my arms swung weighted, my legs floated like a ballet dancer lifted by each steel toe on my boots as they carried me closer toward the vodka, closer toward the bar, just closer to the stool on which I could finally sit and stare.

I could hear Dexter in back of me with all the guys drinking and clashing their beers together. I heard the word "tits" five hundred times like an echo in a conch shell, along with "fuckin' A" and "no shit." I could hear Steven and the other tall, skinny owner (never could remember his name) counting the cash. I smelled dirty ashtrays and spilled beers on damp carpet. I watched the waitresses pull their tips out of their aprons like kangaroos. Busboys started speaking Spanish again with each other and grouping together to catch the bus downtown. Still I sat staring and drinking my vodka and cranberry as I looked into the mirror across from the bar and saw my reflection.

JONNIE
Just remember, Tobs, cold hands, warm heart.

TOBI
Yeah, right, see ya later, Jonnie.

JONNIE

See ya, Tobs. Get some sleep, tomorrow's
Thursday and you ain't seen nothing yet.

DEXTER

Hey, kiddo, where are you going? You're
not walking out to your car alone, those
days are over, honey. Half this city would
like to kill you after a night like tonight.
You never, ever walk to your car alone
from now on, you promise me?

TOBI

Yeah.

DEXTER

That's why we're here, to protect you, you
got it?

TOBI

Yeah.

DEXTER

Congratulations on your first night. You
got what it takes, Tobs, just don't let all
the other shit kill ya, okay?

TOBI

Okay.

I drove home in silence, windows open, cold, damp, night air blowing through my car. I lit a cigarette and drove up and over Laurel

Canyon toward home. It was three-thirty by the time I arrived at my doorstep. The mess from my panic attack and the clothes that had gone along with it lay before me everywhere. I pushed them off my bed to the floor with one sweep of a long arm and sat at the edge of the bed and took off my heavy black overcoat. My pockets were full of drugs, candy, tickets, business cards, Kleenex, entrance tickets, lip balm, a nickel bag in a Ziplock, blow, cigarettes, lighters, clickers, my knife, lists, and hundred-dollar bills.

I lay back on my bed and looked out my window to the San Fernando Valley cityscape and saw them kiss me, shake my hand, and stuff shit in my pockets. Cocktail napkins with numbers, who knows whose number, I didn't care, I just wanted the drugs. Especially the pot. I hated coke, but I figured I'd give it away or sell it. Pot and alcohol, those were my things. I didn't need to go any faster. But getting high—perfect. Perfect, because I had been perfecting the art of smoking since I was ten. It was a ceremony that I celebrated on a regular basis with joy. I wasn't any light-weight either; I could smoke out all night long and keep my shit together. None of that freaking-out shit you'd see many chicks go through. I could handle my weed.

As I peeled off each layer of clothing and closed my eyes to bring them over my head, I saw the faces.

"Come on, lady, what's it gonna take?" the fifty-year-old-balding man in Versace.

"I know we're on the list, my partner called Steven today," the thirty-year-old assistant, and so on.

Each face that I said no to, each face that I rejected, they all came home with me until I said no once more to them before I turned off the light and closed my eyes.

V.O.
The phone rings. I think it's Henry calling

late from some faraway location, so I decide to answer it. It's Carolyn. I can barely hear her. Her cries for help are faint, hard to hear. She is mumbling, but I discern her pleas for me to come over to the house in the Hollywood Hills that she shares with her husband. She sounds different this time, different from all the other cracked-out phone calls late at night swearing she'd never smoke crack again. This time it seems serious. I struggle out of bed, exhausted, get in my car and drive to Carolyn's. I notice the front gate is open, and I let myself in. The house is pitch black and smells of stale air and cigarettes. I fumble for the light switch and see Carolyn lying on the couch, passed out. I find a cordless phone on the kitchen floor and call 911. I wait for the paramedics to arrive and watch as they pick her lifeless body off the couch and strap her to the gurney. I try to answer their questions, but no words come. The winding drive down Sunset Plaza in the ambulance seems like an eternity. Slowly, Carolyn becomes conscious. I hold her hand and utter, "It's all over now, honey, that's it, it's all over, you're gonna make it." And as I stare out the window I think only of sleep. I've saved her this once, I think, but what about the next time? Who will save her then? I haven't seen Carolyn much since our last encounter at the Olive. We've had a few lunches together and a couple of beers out, but both of us are struggling to make our lives complete. We stay in touch via long phone conversations. I had sensed that things were changing for Carolyn. She seemed restless in her new marriage to a rock 'n' roll journalist and unhappy in general with the path that she had chosen. The inevitable seemed to be happening. Los Angeles had taken Carolyn for a ride. A few beers for fun became a few rails. A few rails to snort became a few rocks to smoke. In a matter of months Carolyn had become a full-fledged crack fiend. She was scoring crack anywhere she could. Still dressed in Michael Kors and Calvin Klein, she would drive for miles around Los Angeles during the day trying to score. It broke my heart to see her so skinny, so cracked out. She thinks the cross hanging from her rearview mirror will save her one day. Every time she'd score crack down on La Brea and Sunset, she'd touch the cross before the deal went down. Every time Carolyn would call and I would hear her voice, I was just glad she had made it another day.

Dear Lord, bless all my friends and relatives, please be with me tonight and tomorrow, and each and every day of my life. Tonight my special prayer goes to my friend Carolyn, please don't let her die.

Before I closed my eyes to sleep, I thought of Henry. I thought of the way he kissed me that night at the Chateau, the way his body swayed when he walked, the dancer's pose he struck when he came to a full stop. I saw him waving his arms as he recited Shakespeare. I saw Henry. All of Henry. I missed his voice, craved the smell of his skin and the aftertaste of salt. Where was Henry tonight? How could I find him in my dream? How could I kiss his beautiful lips? I wanted Henry in every way you could want someone or something. I wanted Henry inside of me, over me, in front of me, his voice whispering my name across my ear as he moved his mouth down to my neck. And I missed my secret. I needed Henry to remind me I could still feel things, even though I was selling my soul.

I made a pact with myself that night not to tell Henry about the Door. Henry must not know, I thought to myself, about anything that has to do with the Door. Henry has to remain separate from the Door. He will be my lover only. I will tell him nothing about the Door, nothing about the Story, and nothing about my day-to-day life. He'll never meet my friends, our paths will never cross. I'll see him when he calls, and I'll tell myself I don't love him, even though I do. I'll just want him. Henry will keep me honest, I repeated under my breath as my eyelids closed, weighted.

I slept on my stomach, one knee up, both hands grasping the pillow, panties twisted. Finally, I slept off my first night at the Door.

THURSDAY NIGHT

INT. TOBI'S GUEST HOUSE, STUDIO CITY—MORNING.
WRITING IN A JOURNAL.

V.O.

I think I have found my story. Or the story
has found me. I can see all the faces of
those whom I'll write about. I met them last
night at the Door. It's strange how much
comfort I felt in such a terrible place. Cold,
damp, dark, sinful. How can it feel so
good? Who will I be when all this is over?
How will the story end? I don't feel anything now, I just want to live the story, until
I can't do it anymore, until I have to write
it. I took a Polaroid of myself this morning.
Kind of a first-night-after-the-Door thing. I
think I'll save it until the last night at the
Door and compare the two. I put it in the
picture box. The depression is back. I feel
the black rain coming down. It's like a deto-
nated silence that engulfs my heart and

thickens my blood. All of the traumas of
my past are exploding before my eyes.

*Loud noises disturb me to the point of rage, quick movements in
front of me startle and confuse me, I feel disconnected, as though
I am staring through a window, looking out at life, unseen by the
rest of the world. This is what today feels like, tomorrow, who
knows? Sometimes it stays dormant for years, letting me breathe,
laugh and smile, only to return when I least expect it. It grabs me
hard in my head. I try to second-guess it as only a small setback,
but I know what it is, I've felt my depression before and I know
how it goes. So I think to myself, if I can keep running, if I can just
hold on, maybe I'll beat it this time. But I can't forget, the depression is everywhere. It's there when I wake up and look in the mirror in the morning; it's there in the choice between toast or fruit;
it's present when I decide what to wear; it's there and in charge of
my tone of voice; it's everywhere I go. . . .*

The chances of me answering my phone before noon were slim to
none, but given my new means of support, I was definitely not
answering it. Missed calls were unimportant to me, the sure satisfaction of just watching the phone ring and not answering seemed
so much more powerful that I figured the few and lucky would
eventually find me one way or another. And they usually did by just
showing up on my doorstep or running into me at one of my local
haunts for breakfast. But this morning was different from all the
rest of the inconsequential days that had come before. I was no
longer just another pretty girl living and struggling in Los Angeles
to make it as an actress; now I had actually awoken with a real and
true title, not one invented by me or my alter ego, but a real title
and a real job. I hadn't the money yet in my pocket from a week's
pay, but Saturday was on the way, and the piles of unpaid bills on

the kitchen table would be paid. But now the order seemed to have purpose to its madness and the categories I had selected for them made sense. Rent, Car, Cash. I made notes on each bill of how to pay it off. I made calls, deals, arrangements, payment plans, and commitments with the local utility companies, the phone company, and my patient landlords, who, if they had not been going through a divorce—the typical producer/starlet kind—would have made me homeless. It was about getting through one day at a time.

The next order of business was a trip to the unemployment office. Even though I now had a job, I wasn't about to stop the extra cash coming my way.

INT. NORTH HOLLYWOOD UNEMPLOYMENT OFFICE:

V.O.

I stood in the information line at the North
Hollywood unemployment office, guilty:
guilty of being white, guilty of being able
to get a job but still trying to use the system for all it had to give me, guilty of
wanting more. I hid behind my dark glasses, waiting with the others, waiting in the
line. Aware of my crime against the country, I hid and waited all at the same time. I
prepped myself over and over again with
the lie that I would tell as the line moved
forward, forward to the money. I prepared
the speech and went over the reason and
tried to forecast the questions that might
be asked. I weaved in and out of my mind
the pitfalls that I might encounter should
the unexpected question be proposed. I

searched for the answer, got it, moved on; I examined the interviewers behind the Plexiglas, watching their every move, one being more difficult than the next. I counted the people in front of me and tried to time the window I would end up at; I wanted to choose. I wanted only to get by on my bullshit, to win. How long can I wait in this fuckin' line before they discover me, before they just bust out from behind the Plexiglas and arrest me? I stand in the line and wait. I notice the young Hispanic mothers with their children, the out-of-work actors, the other liars like me. I feel better, I feel worse. I don't feel anything. I wait. I see Bloomfield Hills in my mind. I see my grandfather's face and feel shame, but I still stand. I need the money. I was finally stealing from the government, that was it, getting something back, something I felt I deserved. I didn't care if someone more desperate needed the money, how could anyone be more desperate than me? I liked the line, it meant that I was common, regular. It humbled me. I liked the company of lost souls.

UNEMPLOYMENT CLERK

Fill out this claim form with all your previous employers and their addresses. Have a seat over there in the blue chairs and wait until someone calls your name.

V.O.

Still paranoid that the more time I spent
there the more likely someone might recognize me. Someone from the Door maybe,
or one of my out-of-work actor friends.
Anyone who could call me out on my lie. I
read and reread every inch of the claim
form, checking the legitimacy of my lies,
calculating my false earnings and adding up
the money in my head that would be spent
on all the extras in my life. I added the
money on a weekly basis to what I was
bringing home from the club and figured
the difference between the nights I would
take at the Door and the nights I didn't. I
made averages from month to month on my
personal expenses and the extra income
from unemployment to the exact month
when it would run out. I was running the
numbers, and that's the way I liked it.

UNEMPLOYMENT CLERK

Tobin, Kelly, yellow line.

V.O.

The moment of judgment, but the name I
heard, my real name, sent daggers through
my heart. I hated hearing my real name. It
reminded me of the painful past that I had
left back home. It was so much easier to
live in my reinvented shoes. The very sound

of that name screeched like fingernails on a blackboard, but I had to move toward the money. I waited nervously at the window as the clerk punched up my life earnings on the screen. I wondered if she noticed my Agnes B jacket, if she noticed the highlights in my hair, if she suspected my dark glasses. I wondered if she was looking at my lies on the screen. Ask me, come on, ask me the fuckin' questions and let's get on with it. Yes, I've been working in the last year; yes, I've lived there for two years; yes, I made that much; yes, that's how you spell my name; yes, that's my birthdate.

UNEMPLOYMENT CLERK
We will notify you by mail in two weeks.

TOBI
Two weeks! Lady, I don't have two fuckin' weeks!

UNEMPLOYMENT CLERK
I'm sorry, miss, those are the rules, there is a two-week processing period in which they will determine your benefit.

TOBI
What fuckin' benefit, what are you talking about? I don't have two weeks, I need the money now.

UNEMPLOYMENT CLERK
Miss, if you don't settle down, I'll have to
call security.

TOBI
Well, guess what, lady, I am security. Have
a nice fuckin' day.

V.O. NARRATOR
I slammed my hand on the Plexiglas
window and split. I walked out the door,
pissed off at the world, pissed off at me
and my life, pissed off at my lies. Then it
hit me, why did I do that? Why did I have
to get angry at that poor lady? Why? Why
couldn't I just walk away, why does everything have to be an event, why couldn't I
just walk out and accept the hand that was
dealt, why did I always have to make it bigger than it really was? Why, goddamn it? I
was on burnout, I was coming down, I
couldn't communicate, I needed sleep, I
needed a drink, I'd been up for thirty-six
hours straight, I wanted to have sex. . . .

I got in my car and popped in a club mix and started to drive.
Rolling down the windows, I let the wind blow through the car. I
needed to stay awake. I needed to make it home.

The one phone call I did have to make was to my mother ensuring
me the $200-a-week allowance she sent me via Western Union. Up
until this point I'd actually been living on $200 a week and still
managing to be the around-town gal that I was. I didn't tell her

what I was actually doing on my new job, only that I had gotten a job. I just figured I was saving her from the onset of suburban heart failure and country club shame at knowing how desperate I had become, and besides, "Hey, Mom, I'm running a Door" wouldn't mean shit to her. I just let her believe that I had gotten a job in my friend's restaurant doing whatever, and when I got some more cash saved up she could lay off the allowance. It just seemed like those were the words she wanted to hear anyway, so why not give them to her; she was a million miles away in Florida, had never visited me. I had basically become a disembodied voice on the other end of the phone who called on Thursdays to get the Friday cash. I had gone past the point of restraining myself from grabbing the cash. The constant need to feel like I was riding out the first land grab during the gold rush had become so familiar to me that I had forgotten how to feel thankful, much less experience the actual gift. I put out of my mind each time I spoke with my mother the tired sound of her voice from working the long retail hours that she did, selling shoes at Bloomingdale's, to guard myself from the guilt of bringing yet another person along for my ride. I disregarded the words she spoke to me on how I would have to start supporting myself, that she could no longer give me money on a weekly basis. I would try to stop her each time, as we had the same conversation over and over again, so I would not see her or envision her on her sore knees, bending down to wait on impatient ladies. But there was always something I could use to keep her coming up with the cash—some unpaid parking ticket, some restricted license fee, some past due bill. Whatever it was, I just needed the cash and I needed her to give it to me, and especially now, especially now that I had a chance, a real chance at supporting myself. The more I would push, the more distant we became. If she ended the phone call with "I love you," then I never really heard it, I just said "Bye, and I'll talk to you next week."

Four o'clock didn't come soon enough, and neither did the disco nap that was much needed before my second night at the Door. Same outfit, I said to myself before I dozed off, just different shirt. Set the alarm for six o'clock, shower, dress, and drive to work. Just do it, Tobi, just show up for once. I want to cry, why don't I cry anymore? I wish I could be held, spooned. . . .

V.O.

> I was in it now. Thursday night, eleven P.M.,
> back against the Door, no ropes, Billy and
> Daniel forming a phalanx in front of me, a
> hundred and fifty people pushing to get in,
> negotiating, bribing, charming. Push the
> crowd back, keep two steps behind the
> guys.

TOBI

> Come on, people, back it up, push it back,
> all right, we're holding, that's it, okay, one
> more, that's it, we're stopping, come on,
> damn it, push these fuckers back out of my
> face, set the ropes, call the back door, stop
> the back, cut it. What are the numbers?
> Check the clickers, check the fake ones,
> back up the numbers, start the back count,
> only ins and outs.

I shouted orders like a fuckin' short-order cook in the weeds. Ins and outs meant that for every one person that came out the Door, one could come in, and it sucked, 'cause it was a tough place to be, especially if it was early and your late-night guest list had not shown up yet. If by chance you got hit late and you hadn't saved enough space for them, you were fucked. Now there would be three hundred at the Door waiting to get in, watching your every move, yelling, pairing off, anything to get in, anything to get picked. But I knew Steven was right there behind the Door, waiting and watching every choice I made, every blonde I picked, every groovy guy with a model, and of course mister plain and powerful, whoever that was for the evening.

I chose quickly and accurately, glancing all the time at Jonnie behind the bar, checking the amount of men buying drinks. I stood strong, letting the beast inside of me free itself upon my new playground of power. The idea, of course, being the longer I made the crowd wait, the more successful the club appeared, thus ensuring my job and all the rest of the employees'. I mean, I wasn't sure how long this gig was gonna last, and I definitely couldn't imagine that there would be more clubs after this one. I was pretty sure that I had to make this one last or it was back to being unemployed. And if I was going to make it last I might as well enjoy it.

I moved my arm up to touch my nose, and the whole crowd watched, each hoping that I was about to signal their entrance into the club, their acceptance to the party. I stepped away to the side and told the guys to shut the Door down, hold the numbers, and the entire crowd shifted and turned toward me; it felt like six hundred pairs of eyes staring at me, searching my soul, looking for a sign in my face that would give them some glimmer of hope. The brutal truth was most of them weren't getting in.

TOBI

"You know what I think, buddy? It isn't
your night. You picked a bad night and
there's nothing I can do for ya. You know
what, darling? I can't let you in tonight. I'm
all booked up. I got reservations up my ass

all night long, and I got about two seconds
to tell you about them, so try us again
another night, sweetheart. Okay, baby,
yeah, that's right, that's what I'm telling
you, I can't do it tonight, now come on, I
gotta work. How many you got? Okay,
come on in. Come on, people, back it up, I
need some room here. Daniel, push back
this crowd or we're gonna get busted. I
can't get the ones I need and the ones I
don't want are in front, stretch them out
more and start calling cars for me. If
Bobby's coming in tonight, he's gonna
come in with a few others, I'm telling
you, if I miss him, this is it . . .

After I had an actor in the club, I could shut the Door down completely and just wait for the crowd to dwindle down. I could now
stare above their heads into the streetlights and see all the beautiful colors of the night. I could smell the city air, take it into my
lungs. I could smoke my Marlboro Lights and enjoy every drag.

V.O.

The colors of the night are beautiful.
Taillights passing like glistening blurs, neon
signs shouting out in great greens, oranges
and blues. The letters projecting shadows
on the street. It was a time to walk away
and survey the crowd from behind, assess
the cold and tired souls that stood waiting,
staring at security, staring at us. From
where I stood I could see myself at the

Door. That isn't me, I thought, that's some
other girl, some other invention. This is me,
this is quiet me, and that's just her . . .

                    STEVEN
So what do we got, it's one-thirty and I'm
fuckin' tired already.

                    TOBI
We got seventy-five in and all the A team's
gone.

                    STEVEN
Okay, then trash it, let these asses in and
order some fuckin' pizza and hold the pepperoni, I hate pepperoni.

Finally, we were alone at the Door and in the final stretch, Billy
and Daniel had a chance to talk and shoot the shit and I had a
chance to be quiet. Billy and Daniel knew the drill. They knew I
didn't want to talk. I was sick of fuckin' talking, negotiating, lying,
saying no, saying sorry, saying anything. I was sick of the sound of
my own voice. I stared out into the street, watching the cars drive
by until each one began to slow my mind down, until the rate of
my heart matched my shallow breath.

We ran them out early, turned up the shitty music, raised the
lights, and called for last call. Dexter got his bird—it called everybody "sweetie"—out of the car and put it on his shoulder and
called for the clickers and walkie-talkies, then checked the exits.
The pizza arrived, I was too tired to eat. We waited an hour while
they counted the cash. Piles of ones and twenties were separated
into thousand-dollar stacks, then slammed on the table and

recounted over and over, until their totals matched that of the previous count, then they were jotted in a notebook like points in a card game.

                              BILLY
                  What you got, I got tens.

                              DEXTER
                What you got, I got twenties.

                              STEVEN
                How much did the bar make?

On they went, back and forth, while I sat at the bar with my vodka.

I stared into the smoky mirror behind the bar. Listening to Jonnie talk until all of his words became part of the background music that drifted through my ears. I could still feel my cold hands holding my vodka cranberry, but my soul was leaving and my mind flipped through the pictures of my past. I was somber and gave myself permission to go back, to visit an old place that now seemed so far away that if I could just visit one more time maybe I could see it all differently than before; maybe this time when I'd visit, I'd find something that I could make sense of, see someone differently than the way I had remembered them from my last visit. I wanted to go there again because I was searching, searching for anything that would lead me to a clue or a reason why I disliked myself so much, why I was so unhappy.

I let the vodka drip through my veins while I left my body on the bar stool and traveled in my mind back to Kansas City.

BYE BYE, MISS AMERICAN PIE

It happened two times in my life, with two different men. Sometimes it helps to think of a kickass song like the one Joe Cocker wrote. But most of the time I just try not to think about what happened.

I was there with my boyfriend, River. We had met in Detention Hall. I had forged a signature on a hall pass to get the hell out of math class for a few moments and sneak a smoke out back with the "gross kids" when Mrs. Wathsford spotted me on the way back and asked to see the pass she hadn't signed. So as I was doing my time for the smoke, River was in for pushing Jimmy James too hard on the basketball court during gym class. We were both killing time. So writing notes and passing them between and under the table would have to do until we could actually speak on our first date on Sunday. We spent four days after school in Detention Hall planning our first date. In our last note we planned to meet at The Carousel. Sunday nights, minors could dance in the disco and drink sodas. I would have my mother drop me off there, and River would hitch a ride with his older brother Colin, whom I'd seen once before picking River up from school. Colin was twenty-three. Sunday night came. As planned, I was dropped off at The Carousel and would get a ride home with River and his older brother. I was supposed to be home before ten o'clock.

EXT. STRIP MALL, KANSAS CITY, MO
A nightclub called The Carousel.

INT. THE CAROUSEL
YMCA is playing. The dance floor is crowded with minors line-dancing and making the YMCA dance movements. Tobi and River have been dancing all night. Tobi takes a break from the dance floor when Donna Summers's "Last Dance" begins.

She tells River she is going outside for some air and will return in five minutes.

> V.O. NARRATOR
> I remember the cool night air hitting my damp chest. I leaned on the lamppost to take a break and get some air. I remember noticing the headlights of a car approaching. I was still trying to light a cigarette when the green Opal pulled in front of me and stopped. Colin, River's older brother, yelled from inside the car at me.

> COLIN
> I need to get some beer, you wanna come? What's all the delay about, darling? You afraid my little brother might think I'm fuckin' you? Come on, get in the car, what, you think I got all day to sit out here and waste a perfectly good tank of gas on you?

We're just gonna go for a little ride. What?
You scared . . .

                    TOBI
No, I'm not scared, but when are we coming back, 'cause I told River I was gonna
meet him back at the table in five minutes
and he's gonna be there waiting for me.

                    COLIN
Yeah, well, you want to be in there waiting
for him with a beer in your hand or do ya
just wanta stay out here all night thinking
about it? Now come on, get in the fuckin' car.

                    TOBI
How far do we gotta go, 'cause I ain't
going farther than a couple of blocks.

                    COLIN
Just shut up, okay . . . just shut up.
        (Colin begins to get upset and is clearly
        drunk.)
Now we're going to get the goddamn beer
and that's final. Enough of this shit.
Goddamn it, I hate whiney girls.

INT.—COLIN'S CAR
Colin lights a joint and passes it to Tobi. Tobi inhales the pot,
and Colin puts his hand on her leg. Colin is still driving. Tobi
tries to move his hand away from her leg. Colin is getting
upset that she is rejecting him.

TOBI

Stop the car, Colin, I want to get out.

COLIN

I told you to shut the fuck up, now didn't I?
Goddamn it. What do I have to do to shut
you up? Now we're going into the woods
to get the beer and that's final.

V.O. NARRATOR

We headed toward the woods. I tried to
remember the turns that he was making,
but it was dark. I tried to notice trees, stop
signs, homes, anything that would help me
find my way back if I could just get out of
the car and escape. I pleaded with him to
stop the car and let me out. But nothing
worked. As we drove farther into the
woods I grew silent with fear and watched
the madman beside me fill with rage and
waited for him to make a mistake, anything
to get away. Finally the car came to a stop.
It was pitch black. I waited and watched
for my moment. I stared straight ahead. I
heard a shallow breath ease in and out of
my lungs. I saw my breath in the cool,
damp, evening air. I didn't flinch.

COLIN

Get out of the fuckin' car or I swear I'll kill
you now. And quit those fuckin' tears, right
now, you hear?

(Colin goes over to Tobi on the passenger
side and yanks her out.)

What's wrong, little girl, scared the boogey-
man might get ya? Now help me find the goddamn beer. I know he put it out here today
in the stream to keep cold. Now come on,
get your ass moving. Sooner we find it, the
sooner you can get back to my little brother.
You sure are a fine piece of ass though . . .

V.O. NARRATOR

So as he was grabbing me and pulling me
out of the car, I noticed the keys still in the
ignition. I turned back to look at the car in
the headlights and try to remember the
license plate, but the glare was too bright. I
tore my dress and dropped a piece of fabric
on the ground. I don't know why. Then he
came up behind me and grabbed me by the
hair and began pulling me toward the
stream. I couldn't see the stream, but I
could hear water running. It was very dark.
I remember the smell of wet leaves.

COLIN

Now where is it? I know you know where
it is, where the fuck did he hide the beer,
huh? Come on, you little whore, I know
you and my little brother bought some beer
and stashed it out here in the stream to
keep cold. Now where the fuck is it? Come
on, I don't got all night here, now do I?

TOBI

I told you, I don't know where he put it. I
don't know anything about the beer.

COLIN

Stop your fuckin' lying. You stop it right
now. Now you tell me where that beer is.
'Cause I know you two bought some today
at the Shop and Go.

TOBI

It's over there.
    (Tobi points down the ridge toward the stream.)

I knew that we were at the top of the ridge. I could see the fallen
tree trunk where some of my friends and I had smoked pot before,
during the day. I was sure it was the same place. I thought to
myself, I know the ridge, I know the way the hill rolls, I'll point to
the ridge and lead him toward the edge of the stream and push him
down the hill and run back to the car. I knew I had seen the keys
in the car. They had to be there, I thought.

COLIN

Where over there?

TOBI

Okay, I'll show you.

COLIN

Well, it's about fuckin' time.
    (Tobi leads him to the top of the ridge and
    points down at the stream.)

TOBI

Down there, he put it down there in the
river to cool, just past that rock over there.

COLIN

Take me there.

TOBI

I can't. I'll fall. I have to go around the
rock, but you can make it.

COLIN

Fine, then stay here, and if you think you're
gonna run away, think again. Don't forget,
I got the keys. Wait here.
     (Colin heads down into the stream toward
     the rock.)

V.O. NARRATOR

I saw him head toward the rocks. I waited
for his head to drop below the car lights
and I ran, I ran for my life down the ridge
and tripped. I fell hard onto the ground
and lost my sense of direction. I couldn't
see the car lights, I couldn't see the light
from the moon over the ridge. Then I saw
him. . . .

COLIN

Boy, you sure can run now, can't you. I
guess you knew there wasn't any beer there,
now didn't you. Say it, you fuckin' little

bitch, say that you knew there wasn't any
beer there, say it, damn it . . .

V.O. NARRATOR

He took his hand and grabbed my throat
and pushed me back toward the ground,
and ripped open his fly on his jeans and
pushed my legs apart, ripped my underwear
off and held his hand down on my throat,
choking me and raping me at the same time
as he repeated over and over again . . .

COLIN

Now I got my little brother's piece of ass,
now I got it.

V.O. NARRATOR

He got off me, kicked the dirty leaves in my
face and walked out into the woods. I lay
there frozen in the wet leaves until I heard
the car leave. Somehow I guess I made it
back to the road. I imagine I walked about
two miles until I found a pay phone. I think
I called my old baby-sitter to come pick me
up. She said she wouldn't tell on me. I sat in
school the next day like nothing happened. I
wondered if the blood that ran down my legs
that night was the blood from being hurt or
cut or just the first time getting fucked.

Four years later I stared out of my high school window at the vast
horizon of solid gold wheat fields. I dreamed of nothing but New

York. As my English class discussed Hemingway's *The Sun Also Rises,* my mind created a new room with all sorts of cool people around me. I imagined myself at fabulous downtown lofts in the Village, racing from exhibition to exhibition, creating a storm wherever I went. I saw the glasses of champagne being poured for me as I entered each new gallery. I imagined the colorful artists around me, discussing theories of beauty. But most of all, I saw me in New York. I saw the true self in me being born and coming alive. It was painful waiting to get older, waiting to escape. As I looked around the classroom and noticed the faces of the other kids, I felt a numbness come over me. I felt left out, removed by my own admission, my own passions that wouldn't allow a single teenage thought about parties or boyfriends to enter my mind. I saw over and over again the same scene of my childhood slipping away in a pool of tears and waved good-byes. I heard no sounds other than the dead, silent heartbeat that echoed in my chest.

I spent most of my days reading magazines that I brought from home or managed to steal from the library. I learned what was hot and new in New York and Los Angeles. I read the restaurant reviews, the book reviews, and looked at all the pictures of celebrities coming in and out of clubs, memorizing the names of all the hot spots. I tried to look beyond the actor or celebrity in the picture to remember what the club or restaurant looked like, and I tried to see if it matched the pictures in the other magazines so I could tell where they were going. I figured if I ever got the chance to go to New York I'd know where to go, so I took up the study of clubs, who went there, why, and when. I memorized the who's who of nightlife in the early '80s. I tied it in with the restaurant reviews and art exhibitions and articles on gallery owners and the various poetry readings being held in the Village. All of this information was made available to me by my friendly library, a forged hall pass, and the *New York Post*. So study hour in the library became research hour to me. I was especially curious about how they got past all the crowds at the front door of the nightclubs I kept seeing in all the pictures. I wanted to know how people got IN. I wanted to know what it took to get into one of those clubs. Who did you have to know? So I kept reading and searching for the answers.

It was the '80s: Studio 54, Area, all the downtown action, Danceteria, Heartbreak, gay clubs, after-hours clubs, everybody was going to clubs. It seemed like anybody who was anybody could be found in a club in New York City at one time or another. So that was the way in, I figured. That was my way IN. It was that mainline rush. I was a junkie for it. I would feel that rush when I read about the clubs, and I felt the rush just thinking about them.

I still had a year left at school, but there wasn't anything left for me. The only thing I ever really liked was cheerleading, and they finally kicked me off the squad 'cause I'd slept with my basketball star boyfriend in cheerleading camp the summer before at Kansas University and had gotten the whole team disqualified in the final competition. But hey, who gave a shit, I'd known I was gonna blow out of school that year anyway and hit New York, so a little personal gratification had seemed in order. That's just the way I rationalized things. There was always a plan behind every move in my life, and the less responsibility I had for others in that plan, the better. Group activities like cheerleading camp were only a way to get away from home and set up shop for a while and live in the real world. I didn't need anyone. I didn't want anyone in my life. I wanted it to be just me. Me on a giant discovery tour of life. But most importantly, I needed to prove to myself that all those days spent daydreaming in class about New York wasn't just some fuckin' waste of time and another dream that wasn't going to come true. I needed this. I wanted to get out of Kansas. I wanted to see what was out there and especially what I had seen in all those magazines. It was my junior year of high school and my grades remained the same. Ds and Fs. But at least I was consistent. The only class I didn't skip that year was French. I figured if I was to become a model and someday live in Paris, well, then French would be helpful, so I stuck it out. I hated it, but it was all part of the plan.

After school, on the days that I would actually finish, I had a job at the mall. I had been working in the same clothing store since I was fourteen, having lied to them about my age. I was saving money for New York, at least the money I had left after I bought clothes. By this time I had given up on the high school boys and moved on to college men. I just lied about my age. I looked older, and high school boys had nothing to offer, so on I went. I hooked up with a sophomore guy at Kansas University that I knew through a friend from Catholic school—she used to take me to frat parties on the weekends after work. They worked at the mall too, so hooking up with them was far more exciting than the girls I knew from public school, and besides, they taught me how to pee outside without pulling down my underwear.

V.O. NARRATOR

You are about to meet Missy, Kelly and Lola. My Catholic girls' school friends. I met them all through Missy, with whom I worked at the mall. They were nothing like my public school friends. Missy was quirky; tall and slender with a sort of tomboy harshness to her. She could scare the living shit out of you when you heard\her speak with the voice of a 70-year-old man who smokes three packs of cigarettes a day. She was tough as nails and bossy. I loved her. I thought she could have a great career in the military. Kelly, on the other hand, was soft and beautiful. She was all prep, pink and green with matching monogrammed everything, right down to her signet ring. She drank like a fish, swore like a fisherman, and was the most popular girl in her school. Lola was the blonde bombshell, a pinup girl in every way. She had the biggest tits in her junior class and wore too much makeup. All the boys loved her. She was sweet as pie and could get anything she wanted just by batting her long fake eyelashes. Lola only drank beer and only from kegs. She taught us all how to give blow jobs one day on a hot dog from the Frosty Freeze behind the mall. She had a little library of books on how to do "it."

It seemed like they had a whole network of men at their disposal and in all age ranges. So every Friday night after we got off from work, we changed into the most creative, colorful, pink and green preppie outfits we could get together and headed off down the freeway to Lawrence, Kansas, to a frat party one of the girls would know about through her big brother or a senior she'd been friends with the year before. Away we'd go, with all of our monogrammed paraphernalia, plenty of cold Coors, packs and packs of Marlboro Lights and some good weed one of us had managed to score. On the way up we all had different jobs in the car. I was the joint roller. I spent the whole trip up to Kansas University in the back of the car rolling joints on *Vogue* magazine and shooting the shit with

Missy, who was in charge of music and opening beers. Missy was also in charge of restocking the beer and covering it with ice as we depleted the cooler.

Kelly was the driver, usually because she was the only one with a car or the only one who could find a car to stay out with all night long. She was also usually the planner of the evening. She knew all the ins and outs around campus and usually was the one who got the call from one of her frat boyfriends or some sorority girl after her for rush week in hopes that she would pledge their sorority and give them some of her father's money. But that was never Kelly's mission. She was interested in partying and partying only. Kelly had plans. She knew where her life was headed, we all did, we were just spending one last great year together before things were gonna change. That's what we all had in common. Each one of us had a plan to get out, and until that happened, we just wanted to have fun.

So Kelly took care of the plans and the parties, while Lola passed out the fake IDs and picked out the tapes to listen to on the way up. Each one of us was responsible for our ID. Lola would get them from the senior girls that had dates for the night and didn't need them, and she'd slip them ten bucks for each one. We all had to give Lola the money before Monday, when she'd have to return them. Lola's job was also to inform us how to get into the bar and past the doorman, especially if we were short an ID or two. We'd have to figure out how to pass them back to each other as we passed the bouncer. Lola didn't want anything going wrong with her new ID business. After all, she was doing pretty good on the side with her scam, and as far as she was concerned, she didn't need any fuckups, so it seemed it was also her job to inform us of the ramifications of losing an ID. After Lola was done with the speech, we got high. I got to get stoned first since I was the roller. I couldn't wait for my reviews either. "Great joint, Tobs." "Good job, party girl." "Nice, very nice." Then we'd turn up "Hotel California" and smoke out. Kelly was a good driver, and we never, ever worried about getting into an accident; it just didn't seem possible. We felt invincible, like all teenagers feel at seventeen.

Highway K-10 up to Lawrence was a two-lane highway with no lights, gas stations, rest stops, and few exits. Once we arrived in Lawrence we had to find a place to primp and do our makeup, so we'd usually take turns in the bathroom at Denny's and one of the girls would get an order of fries for us to split 'cause we had the munchies anyway and we didn't want to get busted for just using the bathroom. Lola always took the longest. Who knew what the fuck she was doing in there, but we used to joke about it at the table and swear she was stuffing her bra, 'cause she had the biggest tits of all of us and none of us had actually seen hers. We just assumed that's what she was doing, but each of us had our own tricks in the bathroom. I, however, wasn't interested in beauty. I was interested in weed. The very weed I wasn't supposed to be smoking without all the other girls. So the bathroom was my time to smoke out and get really high. I carried perfume in my purse to spray in the bathroom so the other girls wouldn't know, and then pop a few mints in my mouth. Fresh as a daisy, and high as a kite.

Then we'd rally. First stop was usually a cowboy bar, somewhere off campus, somewhere unimportant, so we could practice our ID scam before the more important college bars toward the end of the evening. We made our plan in the car. Lola would go over the steps of how we'd do things and the order we'd pass the ID down to each other. Then we'd pass a cold beer around the car from the cooler and stuff a few in our purses so we could save money when we got in. If all went well, we were out of there. We were ready for campus, college bars, and frat parties. That is when the buddy system went into effect and all the rules.

KELLY

First of all, if you meet some guy and he
wants to hang out with you, tell one of us
where you are going. Second of all, if one
of us wants to leave, we all leave. Third,
none of us can smoke pot without telling
the other. And if you do get lost, we all
meet at Denny's at 4 A.M. in the parking lot.
Okay?

Off we'd go into the night, each one of us with a different reason
to rebel and a general lack of concern about the outcome of events
that were to transpire throughout the evening. Fraternity parties
were our favorite. All the free beer you could drink, gorgeous guys,
and connections for the year ahead. Sometimes we'd lie about our
age and say we'd come down from Columbia for the night and we
were just visiting our sister sorority, or sometimes we'd tell the
truth, but we always lied about our age. Once we got into the
house we usually had a plan of who each one wanted to scoop for
the night. Fucking was usually out of the question in the beginning
of the night; however, as the night rolled on and the keg drained,
it seemed more like a good idea than a bad one. The question was
usually where and with whom, rather than how and when. So
from time to time, each one of us found herself up the stairs in
some friendly frat boy's room, delivering what the freshman girls
on campus had been told not to do. But we didn't give a shit, most
of us liked sex and it seemed to make for some great conversation
on the way home as we described in detail the different positions
that we learned and how to give a great blow job. Sex intrigued us,
and the more we learned from the college boys, the more we were
a hit at home with the high school boys. It just seemed like there
was nothing to lose. The rule of thumb, however, was not to get

pregnant, and using condoms wasn't an issue or an option. Condoms embarrassed us; we didn't know how to use them or how to put them on, and when we'd try it was always a disaster, so pulling out was the method of choice and taking those little pills we called bombs. Most of us were on some sort of birth control, but we never seemed to get it totally together and were always forgetting to take those fucking pills. Basically we just tried to beat the odds. 'Cause that's what we were doing with everything in our lives anyway, and why should birth control be any different. We just figured if there was a mess-up and one of us did get pregnant, we'd pool our money from the mall, drive across state into Missouri, and get an abortion. There was a plan for everything.

After the frat party, we'd all pile into the car and head out to the bars. This was my favorite part of the night, 'cause not only were there more college boys there, it was dark and loud and it seemed to be exactly the experience I needed to prep me for my life in New York. I had a chance to decide what kind of drink to ask the bartender for, the opportunity to be alone and hook up with whomever I chose, and, most importantly, a chance to watch. I wanted to be the voyeur, to watch others interact while I moved throughout the bar. I wanted to study the choices people made from the moment they entered the bar until they reached the back of the club. I wanted to understand why they sat where they did and why they ordered a certain drink. Just about all of it fascinated me.

I felt a kind of power in myself, a confidence that I didn't have in my life outside the bar. I felt secure in the darkness. I communicated with others in a way I never had before. I felt comfortable lying. I felt relief from the guilty thoughts of sex and drinking and getting stoned. I felt at peace. A dark bar seemed like the perfect place to hide and research all those things I was so curious about in people, so whenever we ended up at a bar, I was pleased, not to mention the last one to leave. But not before I had buddied up with all the security guards to ensure our next trip up would be a successful one.

After falling out of the bars, all were ready for a late-night breakfast at Denny's, where we would make a plan to crash somewhere until morning. We all had to be at our jobs at the mall by 10 A.M. We picked a booth at the back of the restaurant big enough for all the extra people we had acquired throughout the evening, saw how much money we had left, and pooled together to order food. Shirley was our regular waitress, and she gave us a lot of free stuff. Either she felt sorry for us or just wanted us out of there as fast as possible. Whatever it was, we always asked for her.

After breakfast we would drive home or crash in someone's room for a few hours before heading home, exhausted, reminiscing about the night before. The first part of the trip was silent, until one of us would start laughing or giggling to herself and burst out with information on someone else, popping off and telling stories of each other's behavior during the night. This was our favorite part of the trip, and each of us had our own style. Kelly's stories usually included a good sex scenario and meeting up with a potential sorority sister and getting in good with the other pledges. Lola shared her intimate thoughts of the guy she had been seeing for a year already, and they were thinking about marriage and living off campus. Missy and I were usually partners in crime, and our stories about losing each other throughout the evening and trying to retrace our steps to find each other made for great comedy. For the most part, I just liked to listen to the others tell their tall tales. I liked to make little faces in the steamed-up car windows as I stared out at the great Midwest passing me by, all wrapped up in the blankets we had in the backseat, just daydreaming about New York and what it would be like to live there. I knew this part of my life was ending and I just wanted to remember it as it was. I wanted to remember the smell of the first frost on the wheat fields. I wanted to capture our laughter in a little box and keep it close to my heart. Innocence was leaving me, so I just laughed when the other girls laughed because deep down inside I knew I had a plan and that's what I was counting on as the moments drifted by on the long ride home.

THE MALL, THE MODEL AND THE VIRGIN

Working at the mall finally paid off when one of my girlfriends from another store came to visit on a break and asked me if I was interested in becoming a model. I started laughing because I thought it seemed obvious that I wanted to be a model. I thought that I had told my friend hundreds of times about my plans for New York, and it just seemed like the most stupid thing in the world that she could ask me. So after the initial shock was over, she informed me that there was a model search going on in the mall and the winner got to go to New York. All I'd have to do was stand in line and let them take a Polaroid of me and then they'd let me know by mail if I got to be in the contest. The contest was called "Look of the Year," and it was being held by the Elite Modeling Agency. John Casablancas, the owner of the agency, was at the mall with a few of his scouts, promoting the contest and the new modeling school that he was opening nearby.

This was my chance. I hurried back to the store and exchanged my conservative suit for some new Calvin Klein jeans and a white T-shirt and cowboy boots. I ran to get in line with 150 other girls hoping to get the fuck out of Kansas too. I waited and waited, trying to get a glimpse of the faces of the scouts as each girl got her Polaroid taken.

I wondered if I had on too much makeup or not enough. I wondered if I should pull my hair back or leave it down, if I should run back to the store and put on high heels. I just didn't know.

Finally, it was my turn. Confident, as I had been in front of a camera many times already, I posed for the picture. I walked down the long ramp they had set up in front of them, smiled, and winked at John Casablancas, and then took off down the mall back to my job, fearing I had gone way over my break and they might fire me.

Every day after school I checked the mailbox to see if anything had come for me. Finally, after almost two months of not hearing a thing, the letter came. I relished it as I looked at it, with the big, bold, black letters that spelled out ELITE on the envelope. Fearing the worst, I opened it slowly.

"Dear Miss Tobi Tobin, you have been chosen to compete in the Midwest finals in Kansas City on October 23, 1984." The letter explained that I needed my parents' signature on the entry form, I would be expected to attend a photo shoot and I would have to wear my own clothes. The competition consisted of four categories: catwalk, personality, bathing suit, and photo shoot. So I forged my mother's signature, sent in the form the next day and started shopping. I wanted a casual look, not too sophisticated, and I needed a bathing suit to show off my long legs. I knew the judges preferred young, farm-fresh girls, clean-faced and scrubbed, so that was the look I was going for. There was also going to be a big cocktail party for all the judges and girls, which John Casablancas was going to attend, and I knew if I looked hot at that, I was a shoo-in the next day. I chose a sexy little black dress with strappy heels and silver earrings. I was going for the downtown club look I had seen all the models wearing in the magazines I had been reading at the library. The competition was a month away and I had to practice my catwalk, so when there weren't any customers at the store, I'd push away all the racks and make a runway down the back. I'd bring different shoes with me to practice my turns in, and I'd try on different outfits to see which look I felt best in. Then I'd toss on my bathing suit after work while the other girls took over vacuuming for me, and I practiced walking in front of the mirrors. Some of the other girls would walk in front of me and pretend they were models too, and then the other girls would make sounds like there were lots of flashbulbs going off, and they would pretend to be the judges and photographers. During that month I worked harder than ever to save as much money as I could, just in case I got the chance to go to New York.

It was October 1984, and the big day was a week away. I was ready. I finally told my mother about the competition because she had to drive me there and she was my only ride. But I didn't care. All I had to do was win. The contest was being held at the Crown Center Hotel in Kansas City, Missouri, on a Saturday afternoon, but the cocktail party was on Friday night. So on went the little black dress and heels, and out the door I went. I got the car for the night, so I figured I was set. There were twenty girls picked to represent the Midwest, and they were all going to be there, but more importantly, so was John Casablancas. I figured if I sashayed by him a few times, my chances tomorrow at the competition might improve. And I was right. The other girls were beautiful, but most of them stuck by their mothers all night long and didn't have a thing to say except how neat they thought it would be to go to New York. I thought, shit, how "neat" it would be to be able to think that way. Just to have one of those innocent thoughts a year for me would have been a record. And besides, I thought, these girls didn't have to get out. They all had plans to go to college or get married if this didn't work out, but all I had was this one chance, and if I didn't win tomorrow there wasn't a Plan B. I left the party feeling it had been a success. I had made direct eye contact with John and spoken with some of the judges and noticed that I was being whispered about. Feeling satisfied, it was time to go to bed to rest for the big day.

I awoke in the morning staring at the ceiling. The solid white vision above allowed me to paint a canvas in my mind of the day to come. I had been over it so many times in my head that I almost couldn't remember it. But there it was again, me on the runway in front of the judges, smiling as I walked down, turning slowly on my heels, making sure the movement was fluid and graceful. I noticed myself glancing over the heads of the audience as I walked by and not reacting as I heard their whispers. Then came the knock on the door.

MOM
Honey, are you awake? It's time to get up.
Are you ready for your big day?

My mother always pissed me off when she'd say things like that. I never liked to be reminded about the day in front of me, especially what she thought I was thinking of it, so, right from the start, I was annoyed. Nothing that a few more minutes in bed and a quick trip to the shower wouldn't cure. I took the big shower that morning, the one where you actually shave all the way up your leg and then move on to the more private parts. The shower where you use the special soap and maybe an all-over body scrub and then throw on the mud mask and whip up the hair with a deep conditioning treatment. It took about forty-five minutes and consumed all the hot water in the house. Then it was on to the hair, an extra long blow-dry with the round brush, rub in some gel and roll it up in the electric rollers and I was ready for step three: makeup. This is where I excelled. I could do anything with my face. Lift the eyebrows, define the jawline, highlight the cheekbones, make the lips look fuller; you name it, I could do it.

So with my beauty treatments complete and my clothes collected, we headed downtown to the hotel. I checked in, got my name tag, took a look at the runway, went backstage to hang up my clothes and checked out the other girls. All the mothers were hemming and hawing over their girls, and laying out their clothes and brushing out their hair and gossiping with each other. I didn't really know why or understand, but I just felt different. I didn't want my mother to get to know the other girls. I didn't even want my mother there. I was fine on my own, and I felt she was just getting in the way of anything that I might have to finagle. I still had designs to work on John Casablancas in case I didn't win to ensure my ticket to New York, and having my mother around made it hard for me to put on my little show.

After hours of sitting around, going through the personal interview and posing for a photo shoot, it was finally time for the runway presentation and the swimsuit competition. This is where I thought I could shine, especially after all those hours of practicing in the store. We were lined up backstage according to our number, and off we went down the runway. I was near the end and glad for that because my feet were sweating and I kept having to take them out to wipe them on the carpet. Then a sudden wave came over me before it was my turn to head out. Fuck it, I thought, I'm going to New York no matter what these judges say, and that's that. So out I went, keeping my eyes just above the heads in front of me, hoping not to fall or appear rushed, and it was over in ten seconds. I didn't notice one of the judges' faces or even dare to look in that direction as I walked down the runway. Then it was over. It was time to announce the winner.

I didn't win, but I got first runner-up, and they said the magic words: "Come to New York next summer and we'll put you up in one of our apartments and get you started." They handed me my new black and shiny Elite portfolio, and I was out the door. I was going to live in New York, and that was final.

The drive home was grueling, listening to my mother go on about how she felt so sorry for me that I didn't win and maybe if we had bought the other outfit and not such a sexy swimsuit, I would have won. But that's how it always was. She could never acknowledge that my dream had actually come true because I had conceived the idea on my own, and whenever I felt convinced about something she would never hear me. So I fought to be heard that day in the car because I wanted her to believe that I was definitely leaving and most likely quitting school. So I just let out.

TOBI

You never hear me, do you? You just don't
want to hear that I'm leaving, do you?
What the fuck is it with you, why can't you
just hear me? I'm leaving here for good and
I'm never coming back, I've tried to tell
you a thousand times I'm unhappy. Can't
you see that I'm dying here? I want out. I
want a chance to live. I want a chance for
my own life to start. I don't want to live
some fucked-up dream about you and Dad
getting back together and living happily
ever after, and I sure as fuck don't believe
it. So just let me go. Let me fall on my
face. Let me take care of myself. It's not
like you or Dad ever took care of me anyway. I've been working since I was fucking
fourteen years old, and that seemed okay
for you, so what is it? Why do you always
have to do this to me? Why do you always
make me feel so alone and unheard?

MOM
Because I don't know what to say. You're
always coming up with these crazy ideas
about New York and running away and
getting in trouble at school, and I'm at my
wit's end. I don't know how to make you
happy anymore.

TOBI
That's just it, Mom, you can't make me
happy anymore. You can't make up for the
bad grades in school 'cause you can't help
that I'm dyslexic, and you can't make up
for all the time I spend in school suspension
'cause you can't help me to become interested in school. Don't you see, I just want out.
Just do me this one favor and let me go,
just let me go.

MOM
I don't know, I'll think about it.

TOBI
Well, I'm going, no matter what you say,
and if I have to walk to New York, I'm still
fuckin' going.

My junior year in high school dragged on like a prison term. My
only focus was getting to New York and saving enough money to
get there. I continued hanging out with my Catholic school girlfriends and jolting off to the occasional college party, but I never
lost sight of leaving.

I kept in contact with the modeling agency after the contest, and they assured me that everything was in place for my arrival in the summer and that I shouldn't worry about a thing until I got there and they would explain everything to me when I arrived. So at home I kept my mouth shut about quitting school. I figured if I pushed the subject I wasn't going anywhere, and once I was gone they couldn't get me back anyway. My grades had gotten even worse than my average Ds, and I was flunking most of the classes. All the time I had spent skipping class and working was really starting to show. I was on my way out, and I knew it. I kept getting pulled into the principal's office and asked over and over why I wasn't applying myself and why I seemed so unhappy, and as the little meetings got closer and closer to one another, I just let him have it.

TOBI

You know why I hate this school? 'Cause you're a bunch of fuckin' hicks, and I'm out of here. That's right, I quit, you hear me, you little prick, I quit! Oh, and if you think that I didn't notice how you'd always stare at me in the hall, well think again, pervert, 'cause I did. You're the one they should lock up.

PRINCIPAL

All right, that's it, that's enough, you're finished. Go back to class until we call your parents to come and pick you up.

Staring at the clock on the wall, watching the little hand go around and around, I made my plan. This is it. I can't take it anymore, I'm suffocating. I can't breathe. I have to get out. When the bell rings, I'll blend right into the crowd, walk to my locker, get my jacket, and then walk out the front doors. I'm going to do it. I can't take it anymore, I can't do this. I can't sit through one more class. I'm going to quit. This is it. It's over. All I have to do is get to my car without being caught. I can do it. Please, dear God, help me, I can't see these faces anymore. Help me get out of here. Okay, just walk straight toward the front doors and blend in with the other seniors going through, just be cool and walk right past the security, come on, you can do it. Pull yourself together and do it. Just fuckin' walk out! That's right, just walk out the fuckin' doors and start a new life. That's right, baby, the world is your oyster. Just do it, get out!

I walked straight past security and never looked back. I got into my car and lit a cigarette and tore off down the country road, but first I made a little stop-off at the river dam where all the seniors used to go to smoke pot at lunch. They all knew me and most of them were my friends, but this was the so-called loser crowd, the black concert T-shirt kids, the ones who just listened to music all day and drove around in their pickup trucks drinking beer. They were the kids that most intrigued me, because I wasn't one of them. I was the cheerleader with the basketball star boyfriend and all the in-crowd friends. I never talked to them in the halls or acknowledged them in class; it was just the way things were. But after school and during lunch we were friends. So I felt a little farewell was in order.

I stopped off at the local 7-Eleven to pick up a six-pack of beer and a pack of smokes, then headed down to the river. I didn't want to say good-bye, I just wanted it to be like any other day. I just wanted to remember them as they were. I didn't want them to feel like they weren't enough to make me stay in school or that what I was doing was any better than what was ahead for them in life. I felt like they had gotten enough shit from all the other so-called "in crowd" in school, and that me telling them tall tales of how New York was gonna change my life would only seem rude and inconsiderate. So we spent our last hours drinking and telling jokes about the other kids in school and talking about our dreams and what we'd do if we all had a million dollars or we won the lottery and stuff like that, but there was one official good-bye I had to make. I just felt I owed it to him.

His name was Tucker. We had met in math class the year before, and he had been asked by the teacher to help me out with my homework in class if I didn't understand something. Tucker was from the "black concert T-shirt" group in school, and other than being asked to actually speak to him in class, I would never have given him the time of day. However, he seemed like a breath of fresh air compared to the friends that now bored the tears out of me. He wasn't very attractive, but there was something about him that intrigued me, especially the way he used to look at me in class. He seemed wise for his age, and he never made me feel uncomfortable when I was with him one-on-one in class. He knew I was never gonna understand the math anyway, but I guess he figured maybe I could understand him. He made me laugh when he'd tell jokes about his stupid friends and what they thought of me and my friends. He'd tell me stories about growing up in Kansas and running around the countryside with his little brothers and how they used to ranch cattle for a living, but then they sold out after the long drought and now his mother was divorced 'cause their dad had left them for the woman that worked at the hardware store, and just little details about his life that other kids never shared with me. So I liked going to math class knowing that I was gonna see Tucker and hear more stories, and then one day he asked me if I would like to meet some of his friends. Right away the answer seemed to be no, but just the way he said it made the word yes come out of my mouth. He didn't say any more about it after that as the weeks went on, but we continued to work together in class and see each other occasionally in the library, and then one afternoon in the library he came over to my table and asked me to come with him after school. He didn't tell me where, he just said to meet him in the parking lot after school. So I did. And he drove me to the river. And one by one, as he introduced me to the kids I had never said hello to in school, he said my name to each one of them. He didn't have to tell me who his friends were, all he had to do was show me, and that's what hit me. How could I have missed all of this? How could I now accept what anyone said without truly seeing for myself? How could I have been so stupid and simple to have almost missed the whole truth about high school? Why hadn't I window-shopped first before I'd bought it? And that is what Tucker showed me that day—he showed me how to discover things on my own. To take the risk in life. To get out and be a part of every walk of life, including the ones you fear the most. He showed me that I shouldn't fear growth and change, and he encouraged me to believe in all my dreams and not just the ones people expect of me. So his gift to me was the message I needed before I could actually walk out that door and quit. His message to me was clearly, Things are not always as they seem. He used to tell me to look closer at what I already saw, that there would always be something more to find. And that there was. There was Tucker standing right in front of me, something I needed to look closer at.

We met after school almost every day at the river, and sometimes during lunch when we'd skip class. It was a place that we could share together and a place we could be seen together. For the most part, I pretended not to even know Tucker in school except for the time we spent in math class or when he'd find me in the library and we'd sneak off to the theater and make out. But I still continued to date my basketball star boyfriend and hang out with my old friends and act as if nothing had changed. We were from two different places, and coming together was much more important than creating obstacles we couldn't climb over, so we had the river together and our dreams. We spent hours talking about how things were going to be for us as soon as we got out of school, and how we could finally be together and he'd come visit me in New York and I'd visit him at college, but I knew all along those things were never gonna happen, and I didn't have the heart to tell him. Anyway, I wasn't sure he wanted to hear the truth.

Things were getting more and more tense at school, and Tucker knew that meant I was gonna be leaving soon. He didn't want to know when I was leaving, he just had one request before I did. He just wanted me to say good-bye. I think, more than anything, Tucker didn't want to go off to college being a virgin, and I didn't want him to either. He never actually said he was, but I kind of thought so by the way he used to look at me in the library; kind of sweet and curious, but never in a sexy way. I just assumed he was a virgin. It was a cold spring afternoon, and some of the ice from winter hadn't yet melted, so after everybody left the river we decided to go over to a barn we knew about down the road to get out of the cold weather. I think Tucker knew he'd never see me again, but neither of us said a word about it, we just knew that we had those few hours left together. We made love in the barn and then waved good-bye to each other as we drove off separately down the road. His words would stay with me forever. "Things aren't always what they seem, so look closer at what you already see and there will be something more to find."

FRIDAY NIGHT

I woke up Friday morning tired, tired like I had never been before. I felt the tears running down my face. I tasted the salt of each drop that made its way into my mouth. My body didn't move. Heavy from it all, lost in silence, I didn't think about the night before, I just felt it, saw it, and awoke with it.

I found thirty bucks in my pocket, ten of which I needed for gas and the rest for food until Saturday when I got paid. Someone must have slipped it into my pocket last night, I thought, when I was either opening the Door or kissing them hello; whatever, I was just glad to find the money all wadded up in my coat. Think cheap for food—okay, Farmer's Market. I liked going to the Farmer's Market during the day and watching all the unemployed writers and old actors sitting around the donut shop drinking coffee and shooting the shit about the old days or the strike or Canada; I mean, whatever the fuck they were talking about, I was just glad to be watching them and eating, and it was the cheapest place in town to eat, people-watch, not get noticed by potential clubgoers, and write.

EXT. FARMER'S MARKET, L.A.

> TOBI
> I'll take a waffle with strawberries and
> bananas and lots of cream and a decaf cof-
> fee.

> CLERK
> Okay, lady, you're number 56, we'll call
> you when it's up.

What I didn't know was that the place took fuckin' twenty-five minutes to prepare the waffle. Typical L.A. bullshit. They'd let you
starve to death before anyone would notice. Not to mention the
sugar low and PMS thing I had going for myself. *Jesus, it's fuckin'
hot today, how can it be this hot during the day and forty below at
night? I know, it's because I'm actually thawing out.* Then I'd stop
talking to myself, tired of my own voice cramped with bitchy
thoughts and sarcastic outlooks on life, and then I'd listen. Listen to
the conversations next to me, eavesdrop on the woman speaking to
her mother about whether she should invite this cousin or that
cousin to the wedding; I'd notice the white pants on her mother with
the white matching shoes and bag and think to myself, *Miami.*

Then I drowned in the background noise: dishes clanging,
shopping carts being pulled, cameras clicking, tour groups tour-
ing, children running, merchants stocking and selling. And then I
saw her in the crowd. It was Charlotte. She looked different from
when I had last seen her at my party. There were subtle changes
to her hair. Maybe it was the color, I'm not sure. But there was
something about her that struck. I was sure that she could not see
me from where I was sitting, and I was unsure as to how she
would react to seeing me. I didn't know if she wanted to see me.

I didn't know if she cared. It had been months since my birthday party, and we hadn't spoken since. I felt embarrassed. Thoughts raced through my head. I contemplated the words that I could start out with to say hello. I thought of things to tell her that I'd been up to that would explain my not staying in touch. I thought of lies to tell her to make her think I was trying to clean up my act and turn my life around. I thought of the jobs I could tell her I was doing so that I would not have to explain why I looked so tired, but I never thought once to tell her the truth. Charlotte was too clean, too perfect for my messy life. I was a sinner in her Christian world, and I never thought there would be room for someone like me. So I waited, watching as Charlotte paid for her coffee, turned and started walking right toward me. There was no time to hide, no time to run. I noticed her smiling when I caught her eye, and she said hello. I just looked and said hello. Her manners would never permit her to be anything but nice. Charlotte was kind all the way through. She meant what she said and had always been truthful with me about her feelings.

Seeing Charlotte took my breath away. I felt naked, and lessened, like a deer in headlights. I felt busted. Charlotte's buzz kill and my hangover were the wrong mix for any kind of thought process that needed to happen right then and there. I only knew that Charlotte was possibly the one person out there who could save me. I just wasn't ready to be saved yet. For now, I could only see the journey I had in front of me. I thought to myself, *I didn't lie to her. I didn't lie to her. I told the truth about what I was doing and where I was working. Why didn't I lie?* I thought to myself. *Could Charlotte have something, some trick that made me tell the truth, or was I reaching out? What did Charlotte have that I needed so much? Why couldn't I lie to her?* I wondered if Charlotte would ever come see me at work. I hoped that she would and I wished that she wouldn't, all at the same time.

CLERK
Number 56, waffle with strawberries,
bananas, extra cream, decaf.

I arrived home to sixteen new messages on line one, six on line two, and a message tacked to my door from Henry: "Hi, I lost my address book and I can't find your number. I'm back, call me," signed H.

He was here. I can still feel him. He's back. He's finally back. It just mattered that he was back. I looked at the note a thousand times, read it over and over again to be sure it was him, because I needed it to be him. Henry and I shared little besides being in bed with each other, but still it was something for me, and much more than I had ever given in the past, both physically and emotionally. I guess I liked it that way. It was easier for both of us not to ask too many questions, or at least the wrong ones like When will I see you again? or How come you haven't called? Neither of us had an answer for those questions anyway, so we avoided them to keep the ordinary out of our lives. Henry was the only private thing about me other than my real name. He was my secret, my safety, the only breath that I ever took and felt safe about, and yet he hardly knew me. It didn't matter to him either that I kept all of these things about myself so private; after all, he was after the same thing. Together we had an understanding, and for the eight hours that we fucked and slept, neither he nor I would wonder what the other wanted.

Fuck, what time is it? Shit, I overslept. Six-thirty, fuck, I gotta get to the club, what night is it? Oh, yeah, Friday night, it's Friday night. Where's the note, I wanta bring the note with me, I want him with me. Shower, change, bring the note, get to the club, check my messages later tonight when I get home, they're only people want-

ing to get on the list, don't call them back till Saturday, avoid them till Saturday or Sunday. Bring the note.

I drove to work like I'd driven the route a thousand times before, and the truth is, I had, but this time it was different, this time I was getting paid to do a job and not just going out to soak up the city streets and spew more of my bullshit amongst Young Hollywood. No, this Friday night I had a purpose and I was just trying so hard not to screw up the one chance I had at maybe hanging on in L.A. for a little bit longer.

V.O. NARRATOR

It was probably my dreams that kept Los Angeles alive for me. My dreams were everything to me, and for that matter, anyone who came to Los Angeles intent on becoming a star. It was the promise of all the hard work finally paying off. It meant being recognized and being individualized. It offered security and social status. Fame was everything anyone could ever want in life. From afar, it meant so much to me. It meant so much because so few could attain it. It was invented for the master game players of life. To become famous and rich was my goal. Life any other way seemed hopelessly ordinary now. I wanted my dreams and all that went along with them. My dreams pushed me through the days when I had no money and no job. My dreams comforted me when I had run out of excuses for my bad behavior. It was all about my dreams. That's what made me run four miles a day in the hot sun. It's what helped me lie to get what I needed, what kept me going from one moment to the next. My dirty little lie . . . I sought to be around others with the same dream or those who had achieved it. I read all there was to read on becoming a star. I slept with stars. I worked with stars. It was my entire motive for staying in Los Angeles at whatever price I'd have to pay. It's how I justified running a Door. "At whatever price," I would say. It made it easier. Knowing that there was this prize at the end, knowing all my hard work would be rewarded with so many possibilities and opportunities. The future seemed almost guaranteed. I was paying my dues, as they said. Just paying my dues.

DEXTER

Okay, Tobs, Fridays are like this. We're hit early for dinner reservations, then around eleven we get slammed till about one-thirty. Then it's round'em up cowboy, time for us to get 'em out of here, so watch your ins and outs till twelve, 'cause you're gonna need the space, darling. And oh yeah, make sure you and the guys get the pizza money. . . .

TOBI
What the fuck is the pizza money?

DEXTER
On Friday nights we gotta buy the pizza
from next door 'cause they close the kitchen
early so we gotta make the dough at the
door for the pizza fund. You'll get the
knack for it, I'm sure. Come on, guys, it's
seven-thirty, let's get outside. We're open.

EXT. NIGHTCLUB, MELROSE AVENUE, L.A.

TOBI
What's the count?

DANIEL
Ninety-eight.

TOBI
What's the time?

BILLY
10:30.

TOBI
We're holding.

BILLY
We're holding, Tobs, now's the time.

                          TOBI
What time?

                          BILLY
The pizza money, get the fuckin' pizza money.

                          TOBI
I got a club packed with fuckers up my ass,
room for only five more, I got ten reserved
coming in fifteen minutes, and fuckin'
everybody's best friend on the way, so what
the fuck are you askin' me for the fuckin'
pizza money for?

                          BILLY
'Cause you need to learn how to make the
deal, and if you don't learn now, you're not
gonna make it, so do it. Just get the money.

That's when the shit started to hit the fan. They'd wait, but not all
night. So I made deals. Deals based on everything and anything
you could think of. Whatever I had, I used. I made deals for the
next night, for later that night, for whenever I could, I would have
sold any lie they would have bought if it would have just moved
me on to the next deal, and gotten them out of my face. But the
bottom line was, some just weren't getting in.

                          TOBI
          Not tonight, can't do it, private party.

That was my all-time favorite line. That line saved my ass so many
times I can't tell you. There were so many lines. It just depended on

the person you were telling them to. They walked up to me, told me their tale, and I picked my weapon. It was combat, the outcome always unknown, the stakes always uneven, and then the occasional surprise, the easy one. The one that gets to come in anyway, the one that just gets kisses and hellos and where have you beens, yeah that's the one that lets me breathe between the hard work. But the money was the thing. It was what truly fascinated me about the Door. Money in the wrong hands and a reason to use it for getting into something you didn't need in your life, that amused me. It was selling out, and I wanted to watch. It went like this.

Say I turn you away, for whatever reason, maybe the club's too crowded, maybe it's a private party, maybe you're with too many people. That's when they'd make their move to the money conversation. How much? Well, that depended on the person. See, say you start at twenty bucks; shit, that made me laugh. Oh, and fifty bucks—desperate, gross. But if they started at a hundred, we were off and running. First, I'd look them in the eye and say no. See, I wasn't on the take at that time, that's why I lasted. I knew that all the other Doors in town were on the take, but I wasn't. My Door was the hardest to get into and the best club in town because of it. I couldn't be bought.

See, it worked like this if you were on the take. Say it's a slow night, you take twenty bucks. The guy's a loser, definitely, he gives you twenty bucks on a slow night, loser. But you take it, figuring why not, one loser once in a while can't hurt. Well, that same loser is gonna show up every fuckin' great night you're gonna have. And not only do you not have room for him, most importantly, he'll stand out. He'll do something, he'll hit on one of your girls, or he'll say something to some celebrity. Basically, he'll fuck you up.

Anyway, how much they'd offer, that's what got me interested. I wanted to know how much they'd pay to get in. So I'd let them go on, bargaining and begging and trying to cut a deal. It made me sick watching them sell out, but I needed to know the value they placed on getting in, and they needed to show me. My guys knew I wasn't on the take right from the start, so in the beginning it was tough for them. Most of them came from Doors on the take, and they made more money. But I had something more to offer them. The Clipboard. That's what they really wanted, to run their own Door.

> TOBI
> Fuck the pizza money, pizza's on me, I'm
> gonna make this the toughest Door in town
> to get into and by next Friday you'll see.
> You'll see. First you gotta give them some-
> thing they can't have, then they'll pay, and
> then they'll pay big, none of this pizza
> money shit. So just be patient and wait.

And that's when I took over the Door, that very minute. That's when I saw the train wreck a million miles away coming right toward me.

> TOBI
> So you gonna gamble with me or without
> me, 'cause I'm takin' bets right now you're
> gonna be a couple of rich motherfuckers
> right about this time next Friday. So what
> do you say?

> BILLY
> Okay, we'll wait, but you're buyin'.

> TOBI
> You got it . . .

Holding at the door meant a sea of faces in front of me, staring, waiting, talking, smoking, glaring, pushing, and yelling. But for me it just meant having a face of stone, the body of a statue, and the will to wait them out, kind of like playing the quiet game in the car on a road trip when your mother screams, "Let's see who can be quiet for the longest!" I loved that game. I always won.

And as we held the door, I left all of the faces in front of me and looked up into the streetlights. I watched the dew drop down on Los Angeles as the coastal fog blew in, and that's when I saw Will. I'd seen him before, watching me at the Door. I'd seen him Wednesday and Thursday night, and now he was back again and this time he was coming closer toward the line. I pointed him out to Daniel and asked him if he had ever seen him before, and he said,

DANIEL
Oh, yeah, that's Will, he hangs out here all
the time, he's homeless and like retarded or
something, just make sure you keep him
away from the Door.

And just like that, with the same disregard in his voice, he also said,

DANIEL
But ya know, I think he likes you, 'cause we
told him not to keep coming around here,
but he keeps coming back and staring at
you, so do you want us to take care of him
for ya?

TOBI
No, just leave him alone, I'll take care of it.

Hold the Door, don't let anyone in. I'm
gonna talk to him.

BILLY

Be careful.

I walked through the line, eight people deep, toward Will. I could
see him rocking back and forth from one foot to the other with his
head looking down at the street and humming as I got closer. I
stopped about three feet in front of him.

TOBI

Hi, I'm Tobi.

He threw his head back, his eyes rolling to the sky as he half-
smiled and extended his hand toward me.

WILL

Hi, I'm Will.
        (After a long pause, he stuttered.)
So, what's your name?

I said my name again, and he twitched his shoulder again and
rocked back and forth.

WILL

I promise I won't bother you, okay, okay,
okay.

And as he stuttered each "okay" I was so glad Will was gonna be
my friend. Because beneath all those dirty clothes and the worn-
out tennis shoes with holes in the toes, Will was all grace.

I guess Will was about seventeen when I met him that night. He had been homeless since he was a child; he was black and he lived in a cardboard box behind some building; he never told me where, for fear, I think, that someone might find him, someone that he feared, but in those ten minutes we spoke that night, I found someone to help and someone to look for over the faces that haunted me. As I turned to leave Will, he stuttered and twitched out his last sentence,

> WILL
> So okay, Tobs, I'll see ya, okay, Tobs, you
> gonna be here tomorrow, right, you gonna
> be at that Door, right, working in show
> business, right? Okay, then, okay, then, see
> ya, yeah, see ya tomorrow then.

As I turned and began to walk back to the Door, Will yelled,

> WILL
> See ya, Tobs, yeah, I'll see ya.

I kept walking, and without turning around I just put my arm up toward the jet-black sky and waved and thought to myself, yeah, I'll see you too, Will, I'll see ya too!

> DANIEL
> Hey, you know what, buddy, she's just
> doing her job.

> CLUBGOER
> Yeah, well, then why can't she let us in?

DANIEL
'Cause that's it, we're closed.

TOBI
Daniel, forget about him, let's forget this asshole, the night's almost over.

DANIEL
Okay, but if he points his finger at you one more time, he's going down.

TOBI
Call Dexter inside, tell him we got a waiter on our hands and get DJ out here too. I'm gonna give this guy five minutes to settle down and then he's all yours.

CLUBGOER
Hey, lady, you know what you are, you're a fuckin' bitch, no, better yet, you're a fuckin' cunt.

Billy grabbed his hand and twisted it behind his back before wrestling him to the ground. Daniel took a swing, Dexter pulled Daniel off, then all three were punching him. Eventually after a few moments they let him go, pushing him down the street. There was absolute silence between us. Fuck it. We were too tired to talk, too tired to know why we fought. We just couldn't take it anymore. The fight stopped the voices, stopped the rhythms at the Door, stopped the music, and got us home quicker. It just made it all stop.

TOBI

Jonnie?

JONNIE

Yeah, baby.

TOBI

I need a drink.

JONNIE

You got it, darling, coming up.

DEXTER

Okay, check the exits. Steve, walk Tobs to
her car, and I don't give a shit where she's
parked, just do it. Tobs?

TOBI

Yeah.

DEXTER

Hey, it's time, it's time to go home.

TOBI

Okay.

DEXTER

You did good tonight, Tobs, you're gonna
make this the hottest club in town and
you're gonna be famous.

TOBI

Yeah, why?

DEXTER

'Cause you're a chick, that's why, and
you're the only one that's done it so far in
this town.

TOBI

Okay, then tell me this, how long do ya
think this will last?

DEXTER

What, this club?

TOBI

Yeah.

DEXTER

As long as you want it to.

TOBI

What do you mean?

DEXTER

What I mean is, you have that kind of
power. It's your Door and you're gonna
determine the outcome.

TOBI

And what if I don't want that kind of
power?

DEXTER
Well, my friend, I think it's too late for that.
Get some sleep, you're gonna need it,
tomorrow's Saturday night.

As I drove home I remembered the note Henry had attached to my door. I shuffled through my pockets searching for it. I needed to remember there was one truth in my life. I struggled to recollect. Had I gone into the bathroom to call him or had I just thought about it? I was too burned to put the thoughts together. I grasped at each picture in my mind as I tried to see myself calling him from the pay phone in the ladies' room at the club. But I couldn't distinguish one night from the other. Was he coming over? Did I ask him to come tonight? Do I leave the door open, or is he already there? What did I leave out on my bed? Did I leave any clues about the Door? Were there any cocktail napkins with numbers on them? Did I put away the coke and the money and the pot? Did I hide enough? Or did I have to hide more?

Those were the thoughts that ran through my mind right before a visit from Henry, especially the ones about hiding, 'cause I was always hiding something from someone, even if he was the one person in my life that I trusted; it was just more important to me that it stay the same with us and never change. I wanted the arrangement we had together to stay that way, which meant there were rules, and if I didn't follow those rules with myself, then I could possibly allow myself to love again, which was something I was not willing to do. I was not willing to be left out in the cold. I wasn't willing to expose myself. I couldn't allow anything but sex, and as far as I could tell, neither could he. But I needed those eight hours of truth between the sheets as we made love and waited for the sun to come up. That was the one thing in my life that hadn't been corrupted, invented or reinvented by me. It was created by us. Two people with the same understanding about life and fear. We had silently agreed upon an arrangement in which neither of us could be hurt, and that arrangement liberated us. As Henry traveled around the world from Paris to Nepal to Italy, I dreamed of him and his beautiful hands touching my lips, moving over every inch of my body as if feeling it for the first time. *Why did I need him so much if he was only moments in my life? Because I love him, because I love him so deeply, so sweetly, so honestly, so much, that I'd lie to keep him. Why is Henry any different than the rest of the characters in my life that I have to lie to or perform for? Is it possible that I have found someone, that there will be one day of truth in my life that is not conceived of a lie? I don't know, I don't know. . . .*

The only thing Henry knew was that I was modeling and acting to pay the rent, and that is exactly what I wanted him to think. I was embarrassed and ashamed of how my life had so drastically changed in such a short period of time. I thought Henry could only love me if I were the fabulous model/actress that I used to be and not the Door girl I had become. I didn't want him to know where the money was coming from, and there wasn't a way to be found out. I didn't know his friends, and he didn't know mine. We traveled in different circles and avoided speaking about our daily lives so that we wouldn't have to lie to each other. The less we knew about each other, the less we would have to explain when we saw each other. We weren't accountable for anything other than the time we spent together.

The previous three nights working until 4 A.M. were hanging on my body. I felt weak and shaky. I couldn't get the cold out of my body and the sound of the wind out of my mind. It took every last breath I had to undress and put away the clothes, three days' worth that lay piled on my Adirondack chair. I left my black jeans on with my motorcycle boots and a man's undershirt. I washed my face, lit a joint, and sucked the smoke into my lungs like it was floating on a rice paddy in the middle of a poppy field in a *National Geographic* ad. I sat on my bed and stared out on the Valley cityscape and felt the damp, cold air flow through my window and over my body. I waited for Henry. For a hug, for a fuck and the only hours in my life I could breathe easy.

EXT. STUDIO CITY GUESTHOUSE

TOBI
Why are you pissing off my front doorstep?

HENRY
Because you were in the bathroom.

TOBI
So you just piss outside, is that it?

HENRY
Yes, I just took a piss out your front door,
baby.

TOBI
Well, okay. Whatever.

HENRY
Yeah, whatever.

TOBI
When will I see you again?

HENRY
I don't know. I'll call you.

TOBI

Okay, okay. You know you always come to
see me when you're either coming home or
leaving?

HENRY

Really, I didn't know that.

TOBI

Yes, you either have just gotten home or
you're just leaving.

HENRY

Really, that's so strange, really.

TOBI

Really. Yes, you stupid fuck, yes.

HENRY

Ha, ha, ha, you're pretty funny this morning.

TOBI

As well as you are, man who pisses off my
doorstep.

The truth is that I would have said anything to make him stay
longer and not to have to hear him start his bike and watch him
leave. Because as he left, so with him went my soul and any truth
in me that came alive in those eight hours. The sound of his bike
starting was the sound of the lies that were about to return, along
with the nightmare that I was living in and loving so much.

INT. GUESTHOUSE, STUDIO CITY
Writing in her journal.

I slept with Henry last night. I still smell like him. I don't want to shower. I wonder why I need him so much, why it's only him that I love. I hate that he leaves me so quickly and so easily. Why isn't it hard for him to leave? How can he be so cold when he leaves? Never knowing when he'll see me again. Just knowing that he can. I hate the way he knows I'm always here. I wish I were unavailable to him. I wish I weren't always needing him the way I do. I wish I could be more like him. He is so sure that I love him. He knows I need him. I wish I were the one always leaving. I wish I were the one never missing someone. I wish I was Henry and not me. I say his name every morning when I wake up. I say it over and over again. Henry, Henry. It scares me how much I need him. I think of him all the time. Even when I am too tired to speak I think of him. I rest only in thoughts of Henry. There are no signs that he needs me. I look for them every time he calls or comes over. He never says he misses me, never says he thinks of me, never says anything that would make me believe he loves me, but I believe he does. I want Henry to tell me he loves me. Still, I won't believe him. I think I love Henry because he never tells me that he loves me. I know that's crazy, but how can I love someone so much and never want to hear the truth?

I've been thinking a lot about Will. I see him almost every night now at the Door. He waits for me to get off work and walks me to my car. I gave him some of my tips and hope it's helping him. Will is my angel. He watches me all night long from across the street. He never takes his eyes off me at the Door. His soul is pure and childlike. He's the only thing I have now that reminds me one day all of this will be over. The guys at the Door don't like Will. They think he smells and drives all the customers crazy when he yells and waves his arms. I hate it when they are mean to him. It makes me crazy. I found out Will is from Michigan. We were born in the same hospital. I knew there was a connection between us, something deep.

I'm also thinking about when I saw Charlotte last. She looked so beautiful, so peaceful. I wish I could call her. I'm just not ready. I can't stop what I've started. I have to finish this story that I'm living. Maybe she'll come by the club like she said, I don't know. . . .

Stella called today, I miss her. I need to see her. She'll understand the Door, she'll understand my love for Henry, she'll understand me now. I'm glad I have Stella in my life. Without her, all of this would seem like a bad dream. All of her craziness makes me seem sane. Her yelling and screaming at me about this town, about the movie business, about the club business, all makes sense to me now. She's the only role model I have. I've shut out all of my other friends. I can't see them. I don't have time for them. I can't be happy for them now, I can't entertain them. I don't have the energy or the time. Stella understands that.

I started keeping a journal of the Door and what happens there. Maybe someday I'll use it for something. Maybe someday I'll tell my story, maybe someday I'll write my story, I don't know. This shit is all too crazy to even think about now. I know I'm isolating again. I can't help it. I feel quiet inside, sad inside. I'm screaming and no one can hear me. . . .

SATURDAY NIGHT

I arose at four o'clock for a shower, some food and a drink. I pushed away my journal, the note from Henry, the sore feeling between my legs, the tired shoulders and my aching legs, and once again became the new, improved me. I got dressed and drove to Tom Bergins, an Irish pub on Fairfax. I wondered why the inside of a bar in the late afternoon smelled so divine. It was a safe house away from a city that rarely changed, a city that I was constantly trying to change into someplace else: New York, a farmhouse in Bucks County, Pennsylvania, a cabin in Big Sur, a ranch in Montana, a beach house in Malibu, anything other than Los Angeles. So the bar was the backdrop and the drinks were the location. It was all about escaping the madness of the certainty. And I was certain that it wasn't going to change any time soon. Like waiting for parole in five years. I was just doing my time, researching my story, spending my days dropping by the way station of life. Only a few Bloody Marys and fries with ranch dressing made it easier, as well as Mikey, the Irish bartender, and his disdain for small talk and Hollywood types. He, of course, was also an actor. Wherever I went in Los Angeles I met someone who wasn't yet doing the job they wanted to do.

Everybody had other plans. It was a town filled with people who were never in the right place at the right time.However, I had found a way to freeze my days and lessen my angst. Tom Bergins was the perfect place to lose one's soul for a few hours and shoot the shit. The old mahogany walls were covered with shamrocks and reminders of days gone by and the ever-present ones I was still living in. I could lose myself in a green leather booth or sit at the bar and carve my initials into the soft wood. There were no windows to let in the light. Not a thing in that bar could reveal one's soul. It was a cave for carnivorous creatures who needed a place to hide. As each minute got closer to Saturday night at the Door, I shed the moments and hours that had just passed like a dog shaking water off its back. Without effort, almost by rote, I put on my new thick skin and got ready to finish my first week at the Door.

INT. NIGHTCLUB, MELROSE AVE.

TOBI
(speaking with Security)
Pull this shit in early tonight. We gotta
turn this place over twice, and I got every
asshole in town wanting to get in. I want
all the dinner reservations in by nine
o'clock; if they are more than fifteen minutes late, fuck 'em, don't let 'em in. I'm
gonna start a line at the Door early, so
push them out of my face immediately and
keep them about three feet from me.
Watch the street for cops and the fire
department and get on the walkie to
Dexter if you see one. Get the second set

of clickers out of the safe and roll back the numbers and put them behind the Door. Call the valets up to the Door before we open, I wanna talk to them. If you spot the cars I'm looking for, just nod, I'll see them. Only open the Door when I tell you to, and if you see Will tonight, don't scare him off like last night, just let him be. He's harmless. Billy and Daniel, you're outside with me; Steve, you're backup but inside at the bar. Dexter, you're on walkie-talkie, and we'll call in the numbers starting at eleven o'clock. Okay, kids, let's rock and roll.

EXT. THE DOOR

> TOBI
> So what do we got here?

> CLUBGOER
> We've got three.

> TOBI
> Can't do three. *(to another)* Whattya got?

> CLUBGOER #2
> There's two of us.

> TOBI
> Are you on the list?

CLUBGOER #2

No.

TOBI

Can't do it if you're not on the list tonight.

CLUBGOER #2

What if we go in one at a time?

TOBI

Can't do it if you're not on the list.

CLUBGOER #2

Yeah, I know, but what if we just wait?

TOBI

You can wait all night, buddy, but I can't let
you in if you're not on the list. *(to another)*
How many you got?

CLUBGOER #3

We're all here.

TOBI

I see Sean and Harry Dean coming, let them
in. . . . Hey, baby, come on in. . . . I'm fine,
how you doing? . . . How's the movie coming? Good, you playing at the Mint tonight,
Harry? Oh, yeah, sounds fun. . . . All right,
girls, let's go, come on in. . . . I told you,
buddy, I can't do it tonight, you're gonna

have to call during the day and make a
reservation.

CLUBGOER #2
A reservation for dinner?

TOBI
Yes, a reservation for dinner.

CLUBGOER #2
But those girls weren't having dinner and
you let them in.

TOBI
Private party.

CLUBGOER #2
Private party? There's a private party here?

TOBI
Yes.

CLUBGOER #2
So you mean to tell me that if I wait here
all night long and watch everyone that
walks through that door, they have either
made a reservation for dinner or they are in
the private party?

TOBI
That's right.

CLUBGOER #2
That's such bullshit.

And those are the words that Daniel and Billy had been waiting to hear. The sign to step out in front of me and stop him from talking so the rest of the crowd could not hear another word. The idea being, if the person trying to get in was initially turned down, then they were never getting in after that decision was made. However, we knew that they would put up a fight, but it was all about control of the conversation and when to stop speaking that made all the difference in the world. See, I could talk them out of not coming in, but I couldn't talk them away once they were angry enough to wait and watch all the picking. So once I got the sign that he wasn't leaving, I'd stop talking, step back, and close the Door, thus causing the crowd to turn on the guy that created the problem, and out of guilt and shame he would eventually give up. Then I could return to the game at hand and quickly let in five or six people to prove to the others that now no such behavior was occurring at the Door and that in actuality the club was open to the public. However, the people I had just chosen were on the list anyway, and I made them wait for only a few seconds, teaching them to be patient, and reminding them that even if they were on the list, that did not guarantee that they were getting in. See, there were always gonna be people who got bumped for the movie stars (or the drink sellers, whichever you prefer to call them). I liked drink sellers myself. That way, one actor wasn't more important than another and I could let them all in on a good night and not feel obligated to serve one ego over the other. I had to forget the rules of life and every manner taught, 'cause they didn't apply at the Door. So I was constantly searching for new ways to fix the craft, quicken the craft, shorten the blow, control the line, weed out the mistakes, save the space I needed, and make money all at the same time.

Then all the madness stops. I've let the last person in. There's only space in front of me, there's two hours left alone at the Door before I close. There's time to travel, time to think, time to listen to the sounds of the street. I can feel the music pound through the Door and it comforts me. The guys walk around talking, laughing, thinking, eating, smoking. I remain quiet. I listen to Billy and Daniel and watch the street, looking for cops, for the fire department. I listen to Dexter on the walkie-talkie. The owners come out to congratulate me on the successful night. They hang outside at the Door for a few moments. The regulars come out for a smoke and visit with me, kissing ass to keep their spot on the list; valets sit down and wait and count the keys, the kitchen sends out food, the bar sends out shots, I smoke and wait for Will to appear. I get paid tonight, I remember that. I watch Billy speak with his hands and hear his Long Island accent and notice his wandering eye. Early Golden Gloves stuff out on the Island, he was talkin' with Daniel, who just laughed and slapped his leather gloves together every time Billy described something that reminded Daniel of his fighting days. I loved watching them dance with their words, and I saw every one of the childhood moments that each described. I noticed their body language with each moment of excitement that they'd discover in their own story, told over and over again, I'm sure. But even if they were exaggerated, and embellished and added to, it gave them a chance to remember the reasons why they had come to Los Angeles in the first place to pursue a dream. But all I heard in those stories was the undertone of regret. Wondering if it was all worth it. Wondering if giving up that beauty, that family, that home, to chase a dream was worth all the hours at the Door.

* * *

The first week was over. I had proved myself. I would be on my own from now on. Steven turned the Door over to me; he would no longer be standing behind it, watching and teaching. Now it was me who had to make all the decisions, call the times, roll the numbers, turn the room, shut the Door down, and every little moment that passed from the outside to the inside of the club I was responsible for. In one week the club had gone from no line to three hundred people waiting hours to get in. I had done it. But in the same moment, I had sold out. After all, what human being could choose people by race, religion, career, attitude, sex, clothes, or any of the other hundreds of things that made up my mind about who you were? But those are the hard-core thoughts, the ones that you aren't supposed to think about, the ones that just happen to you. They're job requirements. That's what you tell yourself, that's how you rationalize them. It's your job. You just look away when it gets too bad or you're appalled by the sleaze. It's your job. Period. Everybody's in on it, too. Everybody's looking the other way. The guys, the owners, the bartenders, everyone who is anyone that has to do with the club and getting you inside is in on it. But the owners, they were the worst. I knew what they wanted. No Persians, some blacks, easy on the Eurotrash, some kids, no ugly girls, and so on. I thought this was so ironic, considering most of the club owners were Jewish.

But then I'd see my father standing right in front of me, practicing his selling pitch into the mirror before one more trip down a lonely highway across Kansas to sell his new fall line.

DAD

If you can sell, kiddo, then you can sell anything, just like your pops.

Then he'd take his shaving cream and make a hat of cream on top of my head and laugh.

DAD
Remember that, kiddo, do a good job no
matter what you're selling and they'll
always welcome you in the next town.

And as I stared back at him with my shaving cream hat on and my pink Barbie Doll nightgown, I kept those words exactly as they came out, and I had kept them to myself until now. Now is when I needed those words to get me through, now is when I needed to believe that I was just selling this club, that I was just doing a job, just trying to get to the next town, just trying to find my own story.

STEVEN
Tobs, you did a great job this week, your
envelope's coming down with the other
guys'. We'll see you Wednesday, have a
great weekend, don't worry about the fight
at the Door, we'll take care of that guy, he
won't be back again, I promise.

I counted my cash in the envelope the minute I was inside my car alone. Four hundred dollars. It was all there—four nights at a hundred bucks a night, and every inch of my soul to pay my way to stay in a town so bleak, so dry, so bright. It blew my fuckin' mind to realize how desperate I had become and how addicted I was to the pleasure of sacrifice. I could barely drive home and almost lost my way on a route I had driven a thousand times before.

V.O. NARRATOR
I think I'm still talking to myself . . . why

am I still talking to myself . . . who am I
talking to . . . I know this drive . . . I know
every turn on the road . . . every bend. I've
probably driven up and down this fuckin'
canyon a thousand times . . . I wonder how
many times really . . . do the math . . . the
years I've been in L.A. times the amount of
days times the average amount of trips I'd
driven up and down Laurel Canyon; anything just to keep driving home and forget
the past eight hours. Oh, yeah, I just
remembered I think I saw Carolyn
tonight . . . fuck . . . I wonder what I said
to her . . . I wonder what I said to anybody.
Put it in park and turn the wheels into the
curb so I won't get a ticket. Get my hat . . .
oh no . . . fuck it . . . I'll get it in the morning. Check the machine . . . no . . . fuck
it . . . I'll do it in the morning. Wash my
face . . . okay I'll do that . . . I'll wear my
L. L. Bean pajama bottoms and my sweat-
shirt and socks . . . turn off the heat . . . get
some water and put it by the bed. Oh, my
God, I'm fuckin' tired . . . roll over and
turn off the light . . . okay. Silence, with the
moan of crickets.

Still cold from the night before, still tired from the night before, and
still a lot of things from the night before gave me many excuses not
to get out of bed. It was in those moments that I often wondered
how I made it through another day. Starved for love, emotionally
unstable, weak and high all at the same moment.

As I arose, I felt a shooting pain in my shoulder that jolted me forward and sent an exhausted breath from my vocal cords. Standing at the Door all night draped in layers of clothing, underclothes and leather, carrying a walkie-talkie was taking its toll. I felt a twitch in my shoulder as I walked toward the bathroom; I took a pregnant pause to catch my breath and remembered the fight. I took another step forward and brushed it off, it was just pain, I thought, just pain. I knew the beginning would be tough, but I thought I just needed to get into shape, develop a routine. I just needed to get used to the mornings. I thought that I'd adapt. I thought I could trick the pain and ignore it. I could hear my father saying, "Do a good job. Whatever you do in this world, no matter what you do, do a good job. Be dependable, show up, have a good attitude, just do the job." Then a loud Coo-coo-coo-coo, and seven more coo-coos before it stopped coo-cooing, brought me back to Sunday morning.

I knew it was going to be hard to find a place to eat breakfast and not run into someone from the night before, especially someone I had turned down. That was always a pain in the ass, catching them out of the corner of my eye as I lifted the cup of coffee to my mouth or bit into my bagel. Yep, I would say to myself, that was someone I said no to last night. Then I would just pray they wouldn't recognize me without the hat and glasses I always wore at the Door. However when someone did bust me, I got the usual "Bitch" comment as they walked past me on their way out. But dodging people was just another job hazard I had to become an expert at. That was one of the things that I actually liked about the job, the hiding. It came naturally. I had finally found the perfect job for me. All my pretend training from the burbs and country clubs was about to pay off.

So Malibu was the choice, as it was every Sunday morning. The thought of leaving Los Angeles behind and staring out at a landscape covered with water always drew me near. I took the 101 from Studio City and exited at Malibu Canyon. I loved driving in that way, passing all the lambs and cows in the fields and heading into the foggy hills, passing through the tunnel and heading toward the beach. I loved the winter beach. It was peaceful and healing. I pulled into my favorite spot in Zuma, parked, got out of my car and walked toward the ocean, toward the calm poetry that created the rhythm of each wave. If I had an urge it was to pray, to be released, to forgive myself for my past. But I couldn't. I could only stare out at the ocean and feel the mist on my face. I felt comfort in those moments, tucked away in my black fisherman's turtleneck and my wool peacoat and dirty, faded jeans and bare feet. I could see an end to all of it. The ocean seemed to promise me that someday all the pain would end, and I believed it. I trusted the ocean.

The only thing on my mind during the afternoon drive back home to the Valley and waiting for the evening to arrive was the decision where to spend my Sunday night. As usual, I came up with the same idea as the Sunday night before. Strip clubs. I Loved 'em, loved 'em, loved 'em. They were the perfect place for me on off nights. I could be left alone there, and alone is what I liked. I hated being hit on when I wasn't in the mood, so they were perfect for me. I had to hang out. I had to stay up, keep my schedule, keep my hours. I also needed to understand. Understand the loneliness and the self-imposed isolation camp I was living in. But the girls had it too. They had the same thing I had. That "don't touch" look, "just stay away" vibe, "just watch." That's what I was attracted to. I had found a place where everyone felt the same as I did. I just wanted to watch them dance and move and entice and tease, and laugh and smile, and blink and crawl. That's what I wanted. I just wanted to catch one of those looks, one of those looks that said, "Just doing my job, just dancing, just paying the bills, just trying to stay straight." I liked the girls. They were beautiful and simple to me. Straightforward. What you got is what you saw. That was the peace I had. I had strip clubs. The louder the club, the more quiet I heard. A white quiet. A still focus that deadened my soul and stretched me past all rhyme and reason and got me through another Sunday night.

NEW YORK, NEW YORK

In the early 1940s, the Blackstone Hotel was the first stop for single, young women coming to New York to pursue a career in the fashion business. Over the years, poor management and poor maintenance caused the hotel to decay, and it eventually became the melting pot of dreams gone wrong and lives unlived. Most of those dreams were still maintained by women, except now the hotel catered to new models arriving fresh from all over the world. Many times, as I lay in my bed planning my first day in the city, I had tried to envision what a New York hotel might look like. I imagined myself exiting JFK and hailing my first cab. I went over and over again the address of the hotel in my mind, each time trying not to mix up the numbers or see 57th Street as 75th or 312 as 132. I pushed down the thoughts of my dyslexia. I couldn't bear the thought of a panic attack or mixing up the numbers even if I had them written down. I wouldn't show the driver my piece of paper. I can't, I won't, I won't let anyone know my little secret, not in New York. I'll practice all night if I have to. I'll run the numbers back and forth in my head. I'm not gonna screw up. I'll get there. I'll do it without the piece of paper. I'll remember . . . please, God, help me to remember.

I didn't want to show any signs of weakness or confusion when I got into the cab. I wanted the driver to assume I had been to New York a thousand times and there was no way he was getting one over on me. Of all the things I had heard about New York, the one thing that stuck in my brain was the stories of the crazy cabdrivers and all the things not to do when you're in a cab. "Don't look out the windows and up at the tall buildings, they'll think you're a tourist." "Never let the driver take you any ol' route. Tell him how to get there or for sure he'll think you're a tourist." "Always have bills under twenty dollars, 'cause they won't let you out of the cab if you don't have the correct change. In fact, they'll keep your luggage."

I remembered all these things from my store manager at the mall who had been to New York once on a buying trip she'd won as the top-grossing sales consultant in our state. So I figured she had the city down pretty well and knew some ins and outs. After my imagined successful ride into the city, I tried to picture the hotel. I had seen many New York hotels before in movies and on television, but I couldn't really picture what a hotel with a bunch of women was supposed to look like. Most of the hotels I had seen were masculine and distinguished with lots of character and ambience, so it was hard for me to picture what the feminine version was. For some reason I thought that the hotel would look like women lived there, painted pink on the outside or something, with pastel and floral patterned furniture and fresh flowers to greet you at the entrance. Along with a few kind young men as bellhops escorting the women and their bags to their rooms.

The day of my departure finally arrived. It was a hot July day in 1984, and all my savings had been converted into traveler's checks and a few hundred dollars in small bills. My bags were packed, and my ticket was on the dresser with a piece of paper containing the address of the hotel and the name of the woman I was supposed to ask for when I arrived. The only thing I was going to carry on board was my portfolio with the Elite inscription on it.

I arrived at the hotel exhausted from the flight and the fight I'd had to put up at the airport to catch my first cab. It was about ninety degrees and my new fall outfit was debuting prematurely, not to mention the fact that the boots I had saved for all spring were killing my feet. As the cab raced down Madison Avenue, I counted the streets as they passed. Finally we passed 57th Street and got onto 58th to loop around to Park Avenue, and back down to 57th and the Blackstone Hotel. As the cab pulled to the curb and stopped, the driver hit the meter and popped the trunk.

CABDRIVER
Here it is, lady. Blackstone Hotel.

TOBI
Thank you. How much do I owe you?

CABDRIVER
Why don't we call it thirty dollars plus tip.

TOBI
Okay, thanks again.

CABDRIVER
Good luck, lady.

The hotel wasn't pink, and as far as I could see there weren't any young men dressed as bellhops. There didn't seem to be anyone around. Where was the revolving door I had seen in all those movies? Where was the red carpet leading to the door, like the one in the picture of the Ritz-Carlton? Where was the sign for the hotel? What was all that scaffolding along the side of the building? I was confused. It didn't look to me at all like the right place, and certainly not a place where an Elite model would stay. I panicked. There must be some mistake. This must be the wrong Blackstone Hotel. There must be two. I've got the wrong one. I'll just go inside and find the front desk and ask them if I can use the phone.

TOBI

Excuse me, may I use your phone, I think
I've come to the wrong hotel.

DESK CLERK

What hotel are you looking for?

TOBI

I'm looking for the Blackstone Hotel. The
one for models.

DESK CLERK

Well, you're in the right place, what can I
do for you?

TOBI

No, I'm sorry, you don't understand, I'm an
Elite model.

DESK CLERK

Yeah, well, so are most of the other girls
around here. Who are you looking for?

TOBI

Well, I'm supposed to ask for Miss Edith.

DESK CLERK

Well, I'm sorry, Miss Edith don't work here
no more. Yesterday was her last day.

TOBI

What do you mean it was her last day? I've
got a reservation under my name with her
as the contact.

DESK CLERK

Sorry, young lady, I can't help you, we're
booked solid.

TOBI

Wait a minute, I had a reservation with
Edith over two months ago and sent a
deposit. Could you please just check your
books or something?

DESK CLERK

We don't have any books to check, young
lady, but if you'd like to have a seat in the
lobby over there, I'll see what I can do.

TOBI

Thank you.

I dragged my bags over to what appeared to be the lobby.
Reluctantly, I sat and waited. I wouldn't return home to Kansas,

no way, no matter where I was staying. I had made it this far, and no matter how long the old man at the front desk said I had to wait, I was gonna wait. I missed my dog back home. I wanted to cry and I was tired, but I wanted to fight it. I wanted to fight every negative thought that raced through my mind. I wanted to stave off the hunger that I felt in my stomach. I needed to make it in New York. My body sank into the chair, burdened by the weight of my dream. My quiet stare at the frosted glass of the front desk became a backdrop for the visions that danced in my mind.

If I try to phone home, what will I say? If I leave my bags to use the phone, will I lose them? I can't get up from the chair. Am I losing already? Is that it? Am I losing? I can't lose, I have to win. I have to stay alert. I have to survive. I wanted to try to map out my next move if the news from the clerk was bad, but I had nothing. Count the money. I looked for the plastic American Express case with the traveler's checks and counted the hundred-dollar bills one by one, making sure not to let them stick together. It was all there. It was all I had in this foreign city. No friends. No one to call. No one to go see. Just the money. What is taking so fucking long?

In the time I waited in that chair, I saw New York come in and out. I saw my new neighbors and unwanted guests escorted from the building and pushed out onto the street and I saw messengers with portfolios race in and out of the hotel, jumping on their bikes and speeding off down Madison Avenue. I saw life. And for the first time in my own life, I wanted to live it. I wanted all of it. I wanted the dirty streets, the loud noise, the honking cabs, the blinking streetlights. I wanted to rise like the steam from subway grilles. I was in love with New York before I even got there and I wasn't leaving now. I kept my eye on the clerk, watching him every time he picked up the phone, 'cause I knew that one of the phone calls was gonna be for me. That's all I needed. I needed that phone to ring. I needed a room. Come on, baby, pick up the fuckin' phone. That's right, tell me it's mine, tell me I gotta room. Tell me I gotta bed tonight. Fuck, come on . . . pick up the phone. I can't do this, maybe I can't do this. I'm not thinking straight. I gotta make a move. I can't wait here, I can't take it anymore.

Then the silence. I heard nothing but silence. The loud noises were gone. The passersby in the lobby walked in slow motion. The light switch on the elevator lit up with the arrow pointing down. The wheels on the maid's cart rolled by without a creak. The street out front stood still. Where's the hunger? Find the hunger, Tobi, don't do this, don't shut down, don't quit, stay here, stay in the game, wake up, don't go away, come back, it's okay, nothing can hurt you here, no one's gonna find out, look for the light, go toward the light, find a light and breathe, just breathe, don't shut down now, come on, you gotta fight it. You can do it, come on, fight it, don't fall down, fight it off. Find the light. Get out of the box. That's right, talk yourself out of the box, you're in a hotel lobby, feel the draft as the door opens and closes, feel the fabric from the chair on your arms, come on, come back, search for the object that moves and focus, move with the object, come on, get out, listen for the sounds, find a sound, make it real, come on, get out of the box, find the safe place to come out, that's right, you can do it. You got it. Get out . . .

DESK CLERK
There's a share on the eighth floor in a
two-room suite with six other girls. That's
the best I can do, I'm afraid. Of course,
you'll only have the couch till one of the
other girls leaves, but take it or leave it. I
can't give you any price break or anything

like that 'cause they're coming down real
hard on me these days with all the new
rules and regulations for the handicapped,
you see, so what's it gonna be, young
lady?

TOBI
I'll take it. Where did you say it was?

DESK CLERK
Eighth floor, suite 802. Ask for Diane. She's
expecting you. Oh, young lady, that elevator ain't been working in weeks, since all
the construction been going on. You'll have
to use the staircase. It's just past the front
desk on the right underneath the exit sign.
I'd help you with the bags, but my back is
killing me and with this heat I'm afraid I'll
have a heart attack. Maybe one of them
girls will help you out. Here's your receipt
for the rent for one week. You pay me each
Friday hereafter if you're gonna stay. Good
luck, young lady.

The stairs seemed a million miles from where the bags were parked
in the lobby next to the chair, and eight flights of stairs up seemed
impossible. But that's all I had to do, just this last push
and then I'd have a couch. That couch sounded better than all the
money in the world right then, and all I had to do to get it was get
up the stairs. As I dragged my bags up each flight I pushed myself
further into my dreams. Each flight represented another step closer
to the goal. Upwards toward the unknown. Upwards toward the

couch. I was thinking simple thoughts now. I needed sleep. I needed food. I needed to pee. I had finally made it to the eighth floor, and so had my tears. I just wanted my couch.

V.O. NARRATOR

I am dreaming. Winded, I run down
Madison Avenue feeling the night air of
New York pass over me, tantalizing me,
performing for me. I run. I run faster to
catch the night air in my lungs and still
faster to satisfy my hunger and the need to
conquer it. I want all of Manhattan inside
of me. I want my pulse to beat to the
sound of the city. Block to block I run,
marking my distance in fruit stands and
pizza joints, envisioning my dream: top
model, my face on covers and covers of
magazines all over the world, agents and
bookers fighting to have me, wining and
dining me, fawning over me like their new
fuzzy young duckling, limo rides and red
carpets and cameras flashing, fabulous fabrics draping my body, famous actors escorting me. I run faster, faster to believe the
dream, faster to keep the dream alive and
faster still to keep the dream. I run from
the past.

INT. STUDIO CITY GUEST HOUSE
Tobi writes in her journal.

*I saw his face last night at the Door. I
always see something that reminds me of*

him at the Door. I see it in a crooked smile,
when a homeless man shuffles, the smell of
a damp winter wool coat, dirty yellow
stained white T-shirts, thick hands. But last
night, sitting at the bar after we closed, I
could smell Carnegie Hall. I smelled the
wax on the black-and-white tiled floors
above the stage, and the steps that led to
his studio. I remembered his white T-shirt
when he opened the door. It said CLICK in
big pink letters. His French accent was
sluggish but authentic when he greeted me.
I noticed the white corners of his dry
cracked mouth, the girth of his gorged
stomach, and a stench in the air of musty
laundry. He was shooting another girl and
asked me to wait. I sat in the morning light
falling through the commercial size windows and watched. She was beautiful.
Long, light brown hair with color highlights. He shot above her, then moved in
front of her with the tripod, talking the
entire time. "Ciao, bella, bellisimo." He
kept waving his arms in the air and making
grand gestures. Finally, he said, "that's a
wrap" and put his cameras down. I
watched her go to the bathroom to change.
He followed her. I wanted to yell to her
that he was following her, but she couldn't
hear me. I wanted to scream and make loud
noises so that she could turn and see him
coming, but I sat on my stool in the light,

unheard. I saw him push his way into the bathroom and shut the door. I heard the mirror shatter when her head hit the glass. I saw him tie a handkerchief in her mouth and pull it tight. I saw him spread her legs apart. Still, today, it's as if I never left the stool. Like I was just watching and it wasn't really me.

ON THE TAKE

Three months passed before I even noticed I hadn't watered any of my old orchid plants waiting to rebloom. I had completely lost touch with time and days of the week. I lived Wednesday night through Saturday night as if none of the other days existed. I spent mornings recovering from late evenings and evenings recovering from early mornings. My metabolism turned into a late night diner craving only breakfast for dinner and lunch whenever. I grew uninterested in frivolous friendships that couldn't work around my schedule. I let my machine pick up all the calls on line one and completely stopped answering line two. I skipped Sundays in Malibu until I could no longer remember the smell of salt air, and I would now make the drive only if I couldn't stand the sight of pavement and cars and beeping horns. I gave little attention to my own life except for the occasional long, hot shower or mudpack left over from the attention I used to pay myself as a model. I let my roots grow dark, avoiding any chance of having to answer or run into girls from the Door I had turned away.

My phone calls home for money became shorter and less filled with information about my life and more about just getting the money. I needed to disconnect from my past completely. I had created a new life for myself, and I was not leaving it any time soon. I didn't want those who I knew still loved me to see me in my new skin; I thought it would be better if I just dropped them postcards once in a while. I had imagined this journey would involve some lying; however, to the extent that I was carrying on, I could see no end to the tales. I found peaceful moments only in rolling and smoking joints with my girlfriend Stella. Her strong disdain for Hollywood and all the bullshit that came along with it comforted me.

V.O. NARRATOR
Stella was thirty years older than me and had become my Hollywood mentor. She could keep me standing strong when I said I could take no more. She could convince me that the mountain in front of me was merely a hill and, to her, all of my excuses were only excuses for not really giving it my best shot. Stella had been a veteran in the club business for twenty years, and if there was one person who knew what I faced each morning after doing the Door, it was her.

TOBI
I picked up a rabbi today.

STELLA
What do you mean, you picked up a rabbi today?

TOBI
Yeah, he was hitchhiking on the corner of

Fairfax and Sunset, and I stopped at the
intersection, and he ran up to my car window and asked me if I could give him a ride
to the synagogue.

STELLA

So you let the rabbi in, then what?

TOBI

So I start to drive him to the synagogue on
Fairfax and he starts going on about Barbra
Streisand and asking me if I had ever met
her. Like just because I'm an American I
know Barbra Streisand. . . .

STELLA

Then what?

TOBI

Then as we're driving he starts asking me
all these other questions.

STELLA

Like what?

TOBI

Like do I have any children, am I married?
And he smelled really bad, he smelled like
musty split pea soup, ya know, old man
smell, so I had to roll the windows down.
But I got to tell you, I think he was an
angel.

STELLA

Why do you think he's an angel? What did
he do?

TOBI

It's not what he did, but it's what I felt
around him. He had this thick Israeli accent
so I could barely understand him, but he
kept mumbling, "God bless you, sweet
child." And then he went on to tell me how
he had no family left and he was living in a
garage close to where I had picked him up
and every day he would go to the synagogue to pray for the people whom he
loved and get his free lunch there. He was
just so grateful that I had picked him up
because he didn't have bus fare.

STELLA

But why do you think he's an angel?

TOBI

Because there was this light in my car that
was blinding. It was this really bright,
white, beautiful light, and it felt so good.
It's hard to explain, really.

STELLA

So then what?

TOBI

So then I dropped him off at the synagogue

and gave him my last two tens, and he
asked if he could pray for me. So I let him
pray for me, which was weird because he
was praying in Yiddish, or whatever, and
that was it.

STELLA
Did you ask him what he prayed for?

TOBI
Yes, he said he prayed for God to bless me
with a husband to care for me, for children
to love, and good health till the end of my
days. He also said he asked God to protect
me from any harm that might come my
way, and most importantly, to walk along-
side of me each and every day until I could
once again speak with him.

STELLA
Yep, sounds like an angel. . . .

As the fall grew closer to winter and the holidays approached, I
was losing interest in things that had once meant something to me.
I stopped writing in my journal at the Farmer's Market because I
would run into too many people from the club. I wasn't actively
searching for acting gigs, and I stopped reading the trades. My
phone conversations with friends were cut short by beep-ins with
add-ons to the list. Agents who had never returned my phone calls
were now calling to get their names on the list. The job that had
started out simply as a means of support had now become my life.
I thought constantly about the club and how to make it better, how

to increase business, how to keep the line long. I had become financially independent and no longer needed help from my mother; by cutting her off I could keep myself from having to explain why I never answered my phone or returned her calls.

The truth was I didn't give a shit about anybody who didn't understand me. I had once thought I had found the Door, but in hindsight, the Door had found me. What was inside of me now lurked on the outside of me and in every decision I made at that Door. I was as coldhearted as the rapist who'd raped me and as angry as the child that had been abandoned by her father. The job was my mirror. Only now I was in charge of the result; every time I looked into that image I could determine its appearance. For the first time in my life, I had the power to choose. But what I chose—besides the faces that were in front of me waiting to get in—was to be a survivor. To choose each path I would walk down, make decisions without the help of God and turn away from anything that had to do with believing in anything other than myself. I chose to believe that I alone had the power to change anything in my life. That nothing had to do with God.

And that's when I made the turn. Right was faith. Left was surviving. And survivors never go right, they always go left. Faith is believing in something unseen, without proof. Surviving is giving yourself the power and the permission to determine the outcome for every moment of your life. That's what I wanted. I wanted to be in control. I was tired of everybody else having the control. I wanted to live life for myself, not because of what I was supposed to become or what someone else thought I should do. I just wanted my decisions to be heard and seen. I wanted the power. . . . I didn't want to give it to God and his unseen ways. I wanted to take the responsibility and be recognized for it. The good and the bad. Fuck God, where was he when I was raped? Where was he now?

V.O. NARRATOR

The only Christmas tree I could fit through
my Dutch doors was a small planted pine in
a red wooden bucket. I didn't have any
ornaments, so I made a star for the top of
the tree out of tinfoil and hung postcards
from all my actor friends on the branches. I
set it in the window with all the gifts my
mother had UPSd me under the tree. I lit a
green candle from the drugstore, smoked a
cigarette and stared out the window at the
Valley. Most of my friends were headed
back East to New York or Palm Beach, but
I was staying in town because the club
needed me and there was no one to take my
place. I had become an island unto myself,
like the teenage girl who locks herself in her
bedroom to talk on the phone and hear the
same song play over and over again.

TOBI

Give me the numbers, what are the numbers,
what's the count, what do we have in, call
over the clickers, hold the door, check the
clickers, lock it up, get me a drink, no get me
a fuckin' shot, call security and watch that
guy, where are my reservations, fuck it . . .

Christmas Eve I spent with Henry. Christmas Day I cried. The
week in between I could never remember. New Year's Eve I
worked, New Year's Day I slept through.

By March time stood still. There was no sense of movement or growth, just stillness. The game I had invented of "pretending to be me" was no longer a game. Every time I put on my black leather gloves and picked up the clipboard and walked out the club Door, it was my reality. I just didn't need to be on my toes as much. The club was going down. Every night we waited for our last envelope to come down from the office, and every night I waited for the list of security we no longer needed. There was nobody to blame, and there was no saving the club. It was just a matter of time until the last drink was poured and I kissed and greeted my last customer. The heavy nights at the Door went from three hundred people waiting in front to fifty just dropping by to actually see if we were still open. That's when things changed. I made a decision that if I was gonna stay until the very end, then things were gonna be a little different.

The new idea was to mix it up a little before I came in to work. That started the second phase, the old job became a new job, only cutting the edges slightly made everything look a little rosier. I found my favorite bartenders and made sure that they were the ones closest to the Door so I didn't have to brush by one of the assholes I decided to hassle at the Door. Now that they were in, they generally felt obliged to tell me how they felt about me. Of course, this would only ensure that they would never be allowed in again, but somehow that never crossed their minds when they jokingly threw jabs at me. But I wasn't interested in their shitty small talk, nor was I bothered by it. I wanted a fuckin' drink and I had about three seconds to get one before some other bullshit hit the fan, so speed was of the utmost importance and finding the bartender to deliver the juice was even more important. I liked my drinks a certain way, too. I liked 'em in tall glasses, cranberry juice, Absolut vodka, a splash of soda, ice and strong. If I couldn't taste the vodka right away, back it went for a floater.

TOBI
Top it off, baby, I've got fifty fuckin' jerk-
offs outside and not an actor in sight. I
couldn't make this jack-off joint work
tonight if I tried to light the fucker on fire
and held out a sign that said FREE!

JONNIE
You got it, darling.

TOBI
Throw on the TV tonight around eleven, let's
get these assholes out of here early, I'm sick.

On the way over I mixed it up a little too. I'd drop by Tom Bergins
on Fairfax, shoot the shit with Mikey, and drop a few dollars on
some vodka just to calm the soul and comfort the demons before
I'd let them out to play. Then, on the way over to the club, I'd light
up a nice doobie and smoke out. I wasn't any lightweight, either.
None of that freaking-out shit you'd see most of the other chicks
go through. Nope, I could handle. So that was the new drill, trying to "cut the edge."

The late nights didn't seem so late anymore; my attitude was
anything but positive, mostly just riffing on or off, hoping never to
encounter a conversation other than the ones I had to have at the
Door, saving my vocal cords like an opera singer so as not to strain
them during the day or engage them in frivolous, meaningless
excerpts of conversation through my everyday life. I stopped
answering the phone. The tears that used to run down my face
from exhaustion in the mornings were gone. Each night blended
into the next. I had not heard from Henry in months and I wanted out. But the minute the sun went down and the dark glasses

went on, every inch of that night air saved my ass from the daylight that blinded me. Every new joke that made me laugh on the walkie-talkie kept me comin' back for more.

As the gardenias began to bloom and the night jasmine filled the air with sweet reminders of spring on its way, March meant nothing more to me than another month in hell with no end in sight. The New Year had brought more club openings and less business. The dreaded plague was upon us. Our fate was sealed. It was merely a matter of time.

That's when I went on the take. I took big. I took all fuckin' night long, as much as I could. I wheeled and dealed like a game show host. I took from every asshole that would give it to me. Then I asked for more and more until they gave me whatever I wanted. Until they promptly placed the cash in my hand they were not getting in, and they were not getting in until I named a price. The price depended on the night. On a weeknight the price was discounted, but Friday and Saturday—forget about it, it was open season on every loser in town.

At the beginning of the night, we'd call the price, discuss the split, and decide how to pass the cash. Then we picked. Good cop, bad cop. We'd take turns, with the golly gee shit: "The club's packed, sorry, maybe one of my guys can help you out in a minute." I'd set them up, leave the Door for a minute, and then the clubgoer would wait for me to leave and approach one of the guys to make a deal. I was waiting behind the Door when they got in, asking for more, and how they got in. It was a double hit.

We played that early in the night, then as the evening went on, I stayed outside and just started the bidding. One after the next, they'd come and say that they were on the list. I'd say they weren't, and then we were off and running. I'd dismiss them and say no. Then they'd wait, try again with the same story, and again I'd say no. That's when we knew we were on the same page.

CLUBGOER
So how much is this gonna cost me?

TOBI
I don't know, how much do you have?

CLUBGOER
Look, I'm on the list, why don't you just go
inside and check with the owners or the
manager?

TOBI
I'm the manager and I say you're not on the
list. Sorry!

On I would go to the next person, leaving the person I was speaking with nothing to say but to watch how I would deal with the next person. By doing this, I was setting up the first guy to believe that I treated all people the same and at the same time preparing the next guy to watch the first guy get through the Door. Leaving both with the answer no, I would then return to the first guy and stare. Like clockwork, he had the money in his hand, and in he'd go. Then back to the second guy, stare, put my hand out to shake hello, and in he'd go. We called it "monkey see, monkey do," and it worked every time.

I was on my own for the solos, people who came to the Door at the end of the evening, hoping to get in easier. Hoping for some relief in price; however, we were still going strong.

TOBI
Oh, sorry, the club's packed tonight; maybe
some other night, buddy.

That's when he gets it, he gets the signal, but how much is it worth? You see it in his eye, summing you up, as if he was the one to decide the price.

> TOBI
> Well, I'll tell you how much it's worth,
> buddy, it's what I fuckin' say it's worth!
> That's how much!

Then I'd sum him up. I mean, what's this guy's dilemma anyway, what's he got riding on it, and what's it gonna cost him if he doesn't get in. Maybe it's a chick, a business deal, a friend already in the club, he needs to meet someone from out of town. Whatever it was, that's how I'd determine the price. Throw on an extra ten percent just for good measure. That ten percent bought the entire club pizza at the end of the night. Business is business.

I set the clipboard down on nights like that, something I would never do. Those were the nights I talked with my hands, if ya know what I mean. Because I needed my hands free for the take. Most of the time they knew the drill. First they'd fold it lengthwise, then corner to corner, then like a little flag, tighten it to the end and slip it between their fingers and right into your hand on the shake. Nice and easy. But the sloppy ones, they were the worst. Pulling cash out, showing off, talking loud, threatening you. I hated them, but I had to deal with them 'cause not everyone paid. But one thing was for sure. The club was going down and that was just the girl I had become in six months at the Door.

> V.O. NARRATOR
> I was falling fast and hard, hitting the bars
> during the day for a couple of drinks to cut
> the edge. I was looking for darkness during

the daylight. I wanted an eclipse. Total
darkness all day long. Light was blinding
me. It hurt my eyes. I felt exposed by it and
did anything I could to escape it. I wore
dark glasses from the moment I woke up
until darkness blanketed the city and made
me feel comfortable again. I was still hiding, still trying to cover the windows into
my soul.

Tobi writes in her journal:

*My job will end soon. I feel disconnected
from life. Disconnected from love.
Disconnected. I miss Henry. I wish that he
would call. It's hard not to see his face all
the time now. His image is all that comforts
me. I whisper his name when I awake and
before I go to sleep. I think of nothing else
when I'm away from all the craziness of the
Door. I fear the worst will come true
between Henry and me. I am crazed by my
lies to keep him away from me. I don't
want him knowing the truth about me,
about the Door. I feel false and fake pretending to be me. I can't be sure that he
won't leave me unless I pretend to be all
that I'm not. My shades of truth and lies
are blending into each other. My lack of
sleep and my determination to succeed, to
find my story, now confuse me. All the
nights spent with Henry are followed by*

postcards from foreign countries or phone calls from different area codes. At times I feel I've lost him for good, that he'll never come back to me. Someday I'll have to say good-bye, but I can't find the strength to leave him now. I need him. I still want him. I've been thinking a lot about my behavior at the Door. Why is it so natural for me, so inherent in my soul? Why does the night awaken me? How can I be so ruthless?

LAST CALL

The last night at the Door finally arrived. My last night to see Will stuttering in front of me and waving his arms. My last night with the guys. My last night with the pretend me. Finally I thought, I've finished living my story. Why, I thought, as I listened to James Taylor on my car stereo with the windows down and the cool, damp, spring air gushing through, was I gonna miss it so much? I was wrecked, exhausted.

I went through the same steps I always did getting dressed. I didn't change a thing. I thought maybe I would change my hat or something, since it was our last night, but the American flag hat with the Ralph Lauren logo on the back was the only one I ever wore, so I just threw it on again for luck and old times' sake. I could feel the muscles in my face. I felt that tired energy turn to sadness. What would I do now, at night? I couldn't go back to clubs, searching and scoring. The game was over. I was only thinking in questions, not answers.

I put on the last of my gear and looked back toward my bed. It had been perfectly made. My house was spotless. I had cleaned all day. I had organized all of my loose papers, stacked all my sweaters and separated the cashmere from the wool. I had put the long underwear back with the ski stuff and folded all my jeans. I had washed my dirty clothes at the Laundromat down the street and eaten cheap Chinese while they dried. I had focused on nothing but cleaning. I hadn't wanted to think about my last night at the club, so on I had cleaned, every cupboard, every inch of the bathroom, under the bed, remade the bed, reorganized all the dishes. Then barely dressing myself, still dirty from the night before, I drove to the mall. I was still on the high, manic, or whatever the fuck they call it. It just meant that something was about to change in my world and that was how I handled the fear of losing it.

I arrived in the mall parking lot and parked my car. I felt numb. I wanted to see colors, shapes, and just walk. I wanted to think about nothing other than what I saw. I wanted to think about exactly what was in front of my eyes. I opened the door to Macy's and took a breath. I walked through the purse department, then across to the sunglasses section. I tried a pair on. Not right, I thought. Wrong color. I needed the tortoiseshell, not the black. They didn't have what I needed. I moved on to makeup. I wove through the aisles like a snake, my eyes rhythmically moving from color to advertisement to smells, then back to colors. I divided my thoughts as I moved from each counter to the next by skin care to lipsticks, then only focusing on the perfect foundation color. I sampled the soft creams on the back of my hand. I inhaled deeply the smells of perfumes as I walked by the display stands. I tested the wet gloss versus the matte on my pouty lips. I searched for the perfect lip color, a soft, light, natural pink, and I watched as the cosmetics girls came at me one by one, peddling their new products and spraying new fragrances on slips of paper for my purse. They approached me out of nowhere, came around corners, from behind me, and straight at me. One after the other, they exhausted me as I batted them off with answers of "No, thank you," and "Some other time." They were getting in the way. My thoughts, my imagination, all of it was being interrupted, all of it was slowing down my sense of sensory sex. Unsatisfied and still seeking what I'd come for, I moved on. I moved on through the mall, trying to find the connection, trying to find the satisfaction, searching for a fulfillment that would stimulate the visual experience to stop the madness. I passed by each store window, absorbing all there was to offer in the way of visual stimulation, each one tempting me to dive into its distraction. But I passed each store window with a chill. Still my mind was searching, still my mind needed to be fed, and still there seemed no end to the wanting. I continued my complacent walk and stared toward the end of the mall, hoping for some resolution, hoping for an end. I passed by the food court and contemplated putting an end to all this searching by filling up my soul with food, but I didn't stop, I kept walking and walking and walking. Finally, it was over, I had tired myself. I had done the job, I was free to return home. The attack was over.

I arrived home, opened my door, and the telephone rang. I didn't answer it. I didn't care who was calling. I lay down on my perfectly made bed and waited to get dressed and go to the club.

I wasn't sure who was on. I wasn't sure who was left. There would be no celebration, no big send-off. The previous weeks had been hell, watching the club go down and the owners sweating it out. I didn't give a shit about anything except getting the money they had owed me for weeks and walking out of the Door for my last time. I couldn't see what my next move was, I could only see what was happening in front of me. I picked up my walkie-talkie, my clipboard and just two of the clickers. One for the ins and one for the outs. We hadn't used the backup ones in a while. I had stopped at the Irish pub for a few shots of tequila instead of my usual cranberry vodkas with lime. I rolled a big joint in the car with the weed I had lifted from my friend's stash earlier in the week, and smoked out in the Tom Bergins parking lot. I was lit. And lit was where I was gonna stay all night long while the ship went down. All I had to do now was open the Door, something I never did when I first started. I would never have touched the Door or let someone in without speaking to them first and checking the list. But tonight, that was my job. Just to open the fuckin' Door and listen to all the shitty remarks spoken under their breath as all the past recipients of my officious behavior walked past me and through the Door. Each face seemed to carry the same expression. FUCK YOU, BITCH. . . . Every one of them seemed pissed off at me. Not one of my customers from the beginning of the club had come to say good-bye; only the C team, the pissed-off losers were coming tonight. I felt scared and lethargic. I was crashing down from my high of cleaning and shopping. I couldn't get my thoughts straight. I tried to focus on the streetlights, but I couldn't. I couldn't find the straight line that would match up with the shadow on the street. I was sinking. I had two hours until it was all over. Two hours until I got paid.

It was twelve o'clock and Will still hadn't showed. On the other nights that he didn't show to pick up some of my tips from me for food and bus money, I didn't worry, 'cause I knew that I'd see him the next night, but tonight was my last chance to see him and give him my number; in case anything serious went wrong, he could call me. But where the fuck was he? Come on, Will, show up, I need you to show up.

One o'clock came, and still no Will. I couldn't understand what had happened to him. I had told him this was our last week and that I'd give him my number. I felt responsible for Will now. He was my friend and I didn't want to lose him. I didn't care if he asked me a thousand times how show business was, or if I'd seen any movie stars, or if Robert De Niro was inside, or if he smelled so bad I'd have to talk to him from five feet away. I just wanted him to say good-bye. I picked up the walkie-talkie and asked the only security left if they had seen him the past few nights, and they didn't answer back. They had turned off their earpieces. They didn't need them anymore. I turned mine off. I heard the music shutting off as I went inside and put my clipboard behind the bar. I didn't open the Door for the customers to leave; it was too dangerous with all the drunks. I ordered another shot from my friend Jonnie and felt my head drop between my shoulder blades so that I could hear the shallow breaths I began to take. It was over.

The owners came down with my envelope and said nothing. They couldn't. They had their own hell to deal with, and I was just another part of it. I know they were wondering, in the back of their minds, if it was the Door that had put them out of business, if I had brought them down. I could see the look on their faces as they approached. It was the same look they'd given me when they'd hired me. That's how I knew it so well. It said, Every decision you make affects us, so get it right, 'cause our ass is on the line. But the truth was always the same in Los Angeles. Nobody is loyal. And they don't give a rat's ass if you're from New York or not. Nothing lasts in Los Angeles. It's not a forever town. It's not supposed to be. It's all about getting in and getting out with the cash.

I was in between seasons, and that was rough. It wasn't quite the end of spring, and summer seemed like an eternity away. I knew that I would have to constantly keep my ears open to find my next job, and that was gonna be a tough one. Most clubs in Los Angeles opened in the summer or late fall, and the money I had saved could only last for so long. But that was the gig, that's how it always ends. The club closes, the money stops, and so do the free drinks. You're trashed, sleepless, jobless, with nothing to feed the power. Nothing to feed the relentless monkey on your back forever whispering sweet nothings in your ear and planting bits of fear and hopelessness. I would arise each L.A. morning alone without my shield, without my distraction, without the power to choose, only to face the mirror above the sink and see the faded reflection of my old self. I was now staring into the green eyes of my sold-out soul. I was lost without the power. I needed it like a junkie. I was like a vampire for the shit, searching for my kill, something to feast on, something to satisfy the hunger.

I looked everywhere for the same high. I went out night after night looking for the mate to my madness. I fucked strangers I'd never met before, smoked weed like cigarettes, shopped until the soles of my feet hurt from going up and down the aisles of malls. I'd eat all day long, every kind of food I could imagine, then I would starve myself. I exercised nonstop. I ran up hills in the Santa Monica Mountains, ripped off my shoes once I hit the beach and began to run in the waves; I tried anything that would feel remotely close to running a Door. Then I'd shut down for days at a time. I wouldn't leave my bed or raise my shades. I was always thirsty, always wanting cold drinks from the 7-Eleven. I had to remind myself of what day it was by the calendar next to the spice rack in the kitchen. I made large Xs in red Magic Marker and small ones in black. Red was for the days when I would eat properly, black was for the days when I'd overeat. Recording the madness and tracking the progress was what I was interested in. Days and time meant nothing to me, friendships meant nothing to me, family meant nothing to me. No one understood. There wasn't therapy. There wasn't a meeting to go to. There wasn't Henry. There was just time to pass. The pounding sound of my own voice practicing the rap, the Door lingo, my one-liners, and the back and forth of it all still rattled on in my head. I had to keep it fresh, I thought, for my next gig. I constantly ran the numbers in my mind until I could quiet myself to sleep or leave my house. Then I heard the words that would haunt me and fall from the sky like diving black crows searching for prey:

TOBI

Let's push it early, get them in here and out
by ten o'clock, I'm busy tonight, no fuckin'
around tonight, I'm taking in seventy-five
until ten o'clock, then I'm pushin' 'em up to
one-twenty by eleven. Watch the exits and
the back door. Billy, watch the street, left
and right. I want to see the fuckin' cops a
mile away tonight.

On and on it would go in my head. First I would see myself at the Door, then I'd be running the numbers, then the crowd would push in. Little flashbacks all day long, creeping up on me as I drove down neighborhood streets in Studio City, trying to avoid traffic on Ventura Boulevard just to make it home. The club was over, but the nightmare continued. I needed the power. It validated me. It gave me an excuse for my behavior. Nothing could feed the feeling for me anymore, not drugs, not alcohol, not Henry, nothing except the Door.

So that's when I knew, I was in . . . it had me, it comforted me, took care of me. I craved it. I wanted to feel and get as much of that power as I could. And the further away it got, the more I needed it. I lowered my standards to the worst possible level when I called up every connection I had made at the Door and every number on every business card that I had lying around the house to find my next job. Ego was no longer an obstacle. It never is when you truly need or want something. It's simply a matter of how far you're willing to go to get what you want. I mean, that's always the question, isn't it? Well, I was ready and willing to answer that question. And the answer was: I would do anything to have a taste of that power again. Anything.

V.O. NARRATOR

That's when I made the crossover. 'Cause there's always that moment or that day when you can look back and see yourself standing at the fork in the road and instead of going right, you go left. And left I went, happily. I wanted it all. The good and the bad. Bring it on. I'm ready, fuckers. Let's take a ride. But it wasn't the job that I had just chosen at the crossroad, it was the choice between being a survivor or having faith. The choice between being honest or being a liar. And what I chose at that moment would change my life forever. I did what most people do at the crossroad. I chose the thing I knew best, the Door.

I would learn to surrender and not survive. To walk down a road filled with uncertainties and the choice between good and evil. To rebuild a life that with my own hands I had destroyed. To piece back together a childhood filled with fear and loneliness. To become naked before God, and forgive those who hurt me and those I chose to hurt. To understand the depth of the word discrimination and the debilitating effect it had on my life. I chose to seek resilience. To find the truth, to be forgiven of my past, and to know the meaning of love and understand its comforts. To find a place in my heart to forgive myself long enough to learn to love myself, and to believe that peace on earth and goodwill toward man can truly exist. Simply to say this journey would be easy or understandable to anyone but myself would be selfish, but the weight in my journey had just gotten too heavy. I had searched my whole life for the expression of love in people, animals, lovers, food, dreams, and all of God's earthly possessions. But in the Bible, love is taught to be forgiving. It is to be cherished and embraced when it is found or when it is received. But where is it found, and where do you go to receive it? I needed to be forgiven, and to believe love existed on earth. To receive a love that was promised to me as a birthright. I had worked long and hard for the devil and I wanted out of hell. Because if hell was on this earth, I was his gatekeeper. And if there was peace on earth and goodwill toward man, where the fuck was it?

FADE TO BLACK

Five years had passed, and I was still running Doors. I had gone from club to club, opening, closing, fixing, adjusting, hiring, firing, designing, relocating, consulting, promoting, training, producing. I had lost weight, gained weight, changed my style, quit smoking, quit drinking, started drinking, started smoking, lost old friends, made new friends, made love with Henry, had large sums of money at times, had no money at times, adopted a dog, moved four times, got sued, went to jail once, lost my house in an earthquake, started exercising, stopped exercising, got saved, found Jesus, lost Jesus, then found Him again, started writing, stopped writing, still made my Sunday list of all the good and bad, discovered frozen yogurt with Oreos, discovered Chez Jay, helped Stella move, saw Carolyn get sober, kept tabs on my grandmother's Alzheimer's, went to Palm Beach for every holiday, learned computers, celebrated five birthdays five different ways with five different groups of friends, started a baby skin care company, sold all my stocks, never had an honest relationship with anyone except Henry and still I lied to him, wrote poetry, called to make an appointment with a therapist a thousand times and canceled the day of it. The only thing constant in my life was the Door.

It was my last week at the Door, and if you had asked me on Monday if Saturday was gonna be my last night to stand in front of a Door, I would have told you to fuck off. 'Cause on Monday I had no plans of leaving, and that little episode where I tried to kill myself the night before I just chalked up to a bad day, and being naked in the bathtub with no water and a loaded gun somehow hadn't fazed me when I'd awoken the next morning still alive, with the clip on the bathroom floor. I'd merely popped the clip back in, gotten dressed, and gone to breakfast like nothing had ever happened. 'Cause that's what you do when the end is near. You never give up, you never give in, you just keep moving until someone ends it for you. I was trying to feel, feel anything, have an emotion, laugh, cry, I didn't give a fuck. I was waking up each morning with less and less of me left, so I was trying to find something, anything, to get my attention back on me and away from the Door. But nothing could stop the madness and my desire to keep the power close. Nobody could tell me I was slipping, 'cause I didn't want to lose. I thought giving in was losing. I thought quitting was losing. I just didn't want to close one more club, say good-bye to another team of guys, see the owners' faces on the last night, watch the bartenders cash out the bar, watch the DJ pack up his records, watch the lights and sound systems being torn down, saying good-bye to all the customers, find another job. I just couldn't, I had to make this club work, I just had to. . . .

That's right! "Hype it up and sell it." "Welcome to America!" The land of the free and home of the brave. It's catchy, it travels, it spreads like wildfire, come on, buy it, why not? You need it, you want it, so go on, give yourself that little treat, come on, get in the game, damn it! So that's how it all starts, all the gigs were the same. Club after club, they all had the same ol' shit to say.

"It's a new club, new attitude, new space, new, new, new . . ."

"Whoopee, yeah! We're gonna kick ass this time. How can we

go wrong? Look at what we got here! Fuck, if this doesn't make
'em happy, what will?"

V.O. NARRATOR

So that was the bullshit that you had to listen to every damn time a new gig came to
town. They were gonna be different. They
had the new "Recipe for Destruction."
"Come and get it," they'd yell as the paint
was still drying on the dance floor walls.
"We found what's gonna make you happy.
We're the fuckin' trailblazers of fun. We
wrote the book on fun, damn it, just come
on down and check us out and you'll see."
The same old bullshit over and over on
every phone call I had with every owner
that wanted me to run their Door. Then I'd
bullshit them back with my little rap on
running the Door and what my team could
get you. I was never hired, however, on the
first week, 'cause that's rookie week. That's
when they try out all the cheaper Doormen
and think they can do it all on their own;
then like clockwork, the phone is ringing
off the hook with them trying to reach you,
and by that time they'll pay you anything to
save their investment, which, by the way, is
always the best way to enter into any kind
of negotiation. I had put in my five years at
the Door in Los Angeles and this time I
wasn't gonna get screwed. I wanted out of
Doors, I wanted out of clubs, I just wanted

out, period. But every time I said yes to
another club, I said no to ever changing my
ways.

Meeting up with the guys on the first night was the hardest.
'Cause the first thing out of your mouth was the last thing you
said at the first club you ever did. "This is my last gig for sure, no
more." But I said it every time I ever did a new club, and so did
everybody else. So you're a repeat offender. But it drags you in, all
the hype, the power, the promises, the money. The reasons never
changed, only the times changed. But it's the same with everything. The Door wasn't anything different from anything else in
life. It just offered the same crime that I knew how to commit and
the same sentence that I was gonna get at the end anyway. The
meals were great, the guys were gonna be there, so what the fuck,
why not, I figured.

But getting in with the guys, that was the first thing I'd have to
do at a new club, and this time it was the hardest. Most of them
were new and didn't know me, and the old ones from the big clubs
were jaded, fuckin' jaded. They were pissed off before we started.
Some of them knew the rumors about me, knew the drill, knew
how I worked it, but the others, I had to get past their macho shit,
and it wasn't easy this time. I wanted out before I even started, and
a new team of twenty-five men wasn't what I had in mind.

Times had changed. The little clubs weren't makin' it, so the big
ones came in. Capacity of up to a thousand, packed at fourteen
hundred, danger zone around fifteen hundred. Waiting lines outside of six hundred for three hours. I was crazy. I had twenty-five
security guys, four undercover moonlighting cops from LAPD, six
blocks of ropes, front doors, back doors, kitchen doors, upstairs,
downstairs, dance floors, side doors, you name it, we had it, and
the loudest fuckin' music you've ever heard, and all of it was on

line one with me. The crowds were like nothing I had ever seen before. The crowds came in waves down the street. Groups of ten and fifteen, one after another. Early, too. Not like the old days when they'd at least wait till after ten-thirty. No, this crowd wanted in at nine o'clock, and they wanted to party. . . . I mean, everything was different. I didn't just have one Door, I had two Doors. Back Door was the front, and front Door was the back. I ran them both on the walkie-talkie. Back Door had me and two guys in the ropes. Then there were three guys outside the ropes and two more in front of the cashier down a stretch from me at the end of the walkway. So there were seven guys just at the back Door.

Front Door I ran by walkie-talkie. Line one was just for me and the front Door. Line two was for me and security; all of us were on line two, and so was every other person's life in L.A. Early in the evening while we were setting up and pulling the ropes out, the hot topic was usually who was fucking whom, then we moved on to the hockey scores, then back to last night's best set of tits, then maybe a few restaurant reviews, and who ate what for dinner, then we'd usually round off the evening with a few dirty jokes and off we'd go. But line two was serious and all the guys knew it. Line two was our lifeline. I ran the numbers on line two and did the club and security checks every ten minutes until we'd close, so line two only had comedy associated with it early in the evening 'cause the rest of the time it was serious. When I did the security checks, I did call-ins.

TOBI

I call your name, you say okay. You don't
say okay, there's a problem. I don't hesitate
to send the closest guy to you to check, but
if you don't have a problem when we get
there, you're gonna wish you did. Those of

. you guys that are new, stay off the line, let
the pinners talk when I call for the numbers. Only say okay if I call your location.

The pinners were the guys who could pin down a larger area of the
club. They were security with a lot of experience, and, most important, they could see a fight happening a mile away. For that reason,
line two was a fight line as well. "Upstairs" meant the action was
on the second floor, and "dance floor" meant center of the dance
floor; the entire club had location calls, and if any of the locations
were called out over line two, that meant a fight. Choosing who
went was my responsibility, and it wasn't always the guy closest. I
chose the guy next to the location, usually, and kept the guy at the
exact location free to cover any other fights that were a spin-off of
the first one.

So my walkie-talkie was it, my only access to the action. Every
sound, every word spoken on that line after nine o'clock was crit-
ical. Line two never changed. It was always the lifeline. After we
closed down for the night, we'd use it to call in the numbers, check
the bathrooms, check out the bartenders, walk the waitresses to
their cars, pull in the ropes, walk down the club, and order pizza.
After we ate, security checked in the walkie-talkies, and I counted
out the cash and passed out the envelopes and we all walked out
together. That was the drill, night after night, unless we had a
fight, then we'd fill out the police reports, go over the accident,
check the bruises, fix the bloody noses, clean the scrapes, and
move on.

There was more than just the Door, however, that made each
club rock. And they were all over the joint. The lovely staff. The
angry bartenders, the bitchy waitress, the fucked-up wanna-be-
Doormen owners, the pissed-off Mexican busboys. Or how about
the visiting DJ, now there's a joy of a human being. DJs. Gotta love

them, hauling in their shit all night long, case after case of who knows what records, and pumping the music louder as the fights broke out, yeah, gotta love them. Those fuckin' little rats. We used to hate them. They'd lock themselves in the booth all night long and flip us off when we'd yell at the little bastards to cut the music, but on they'd play, just wiggin' out to their very own club mix. Shit, it exhausts me to describe the staff, they were always so fucked up.

So where did we fit in? Nowhere. We were separate. Very separate. The Door and security got paid cash. All cash. We were an all-cash business. So basically we didn't exist. Therefore, we were entitled to our own show. We made all our own rules, set our own schedules, and off we'd go. But there was no PMA with this crew. No, we were more like the "Crew of the Sinking Ship," navigating you to and through your own destructive little habits and helping you along the way to the end result. Closing time. But we'd be there for you, too . . . 'cause we had feelings too! We could bail you out if you needed it. We'd just rip you off! Like a bunch of thieves in the night, you'd never know what happened. That's how it went, every damn time, after all the fluff and excitement of opening week was over, it was just another club in a town of junkies trying to stay afloat.

The one thing that seldom changed was the list and someone's status on it. I hated to see a name on the list change, 'cause it wasn't just a name, it was a person, a job, a lifestyle, a movie, a girlfriend, a studio, everything that they had that put them on the list in the first place. I hated crossing off names, the ones who didn't cut it, the ones with the big job, the big movie, the car, the girls. But then the movies stop grossing. The big job goes to the other guy, and the girl stops giving two shits about you and you're back to being a stockbroker. Worst of all, you're off the list. Just like that. No failures allowed. Stinks up the room too much, makes the others feel uncomfortable and reminds them how easily it could happen to them. Only success and power keep you on the list. That's what the room was all about. It was about fuckin' success and power, and that was my specialty, keeping the room stocked with power players. Gwyneth Paltrow, John Cusack, Julia Roberts, Robert Downey Jr., Al Pacino, Sharon Stone, Sean Penn, Martin Scorsese, Robert De Niro, Bono, Edward Norton, Ed Burns, David Spade, Adam Sandler, Jim Carrey, Tony Scott, and all the others. . . .

To keep them coming through the door, first I'd space them out, a couple of heavy hitters like Robin Williams and Oliver Stone, then some girls, throw in a few of the others waiting in line and start the night. But I had to keep it going like that all night, so I kept 'em coming like fire bombs. Boom, then boom again, then drizzle in a few of the loners, then give it a rest. Then hit them again, boom! So I needed them all. The famous, the smart, the beautiful, the creative, the scruffy, the loner, the older one, the younger one, the tits, the druggies, the rockers, the writers, the friends of, the partner of, the guru of, all of them, they all had it. That's what made it. That was running the numbers. It was timing. That's what kept them coming back.

My job was not to feel. Anything. One way or the other. It was my job to let them feel. You're dead in the water if you get emotional, 'cause that's the end of it. That's when you say it's over. I used to test it from time to time, however, just to make sure I was still the cold bitch I thought I was. A couple of times I did something uncharacteristic for a work night, like give some homeless guy one of my tips, or let some loser in that I wouldn't have otherwise, maybe keep a promise I'd made at the Door from the night before, just to check the pulse. That side just slips away. You discover you're as numb as the hooker that just walked by. And every time you think you're gonna check it again, you don't 'cause the idea just gets you down, and it takes you further and further away, so you just stop checkin'. What's the point? What are you gonna find out anyway? That you're a heartless bitch? That you sold out? Or was I gonna find out the truth about myself, that I wasn't as tough as I thought I was? Either way, I just didn't want to know the answer, 'cause I wasn't ready to accept the responsibility for anything.

V.O. NARRATOR

It was a Saturday night like any other. All day I had been feeling something changing inside of me, something beautiful, something inexplicable. For weeks I had felt terribly empty. I heard and saw things happening around me, but didn't feel connected to any of it. I was observing, waiting for this feeling to pass. Reaching out to friends and family wasn't helping. I felt unheard and misunderstood. I was losing control of my life yet still believed I was in control. All the days that had led up to Saturday night had left me with clues; however, I had chosen to ignore them. I didn't want things to change, I hated change. It confused me. I associated it with being abandoned. Even though I was screaming for release inside, outwardly I could never show it. I was too proud to quit, too smart to lose, too beautiful to cry, too lonely to reach out, too scared to stop the pain I felt I deserved for being abandoned by my father. But then I'd see it, in a smile, in a movie, in a store window. I'd

watch it in a restaurant, notice it in a walk,
see it on a sunny day, find it on the beach,
feel it when I heard Henry's voice, smell it
when I'd buy flowers on Sunday morning at
the swap meet, and sometimes I'd hear it in
myself. It was new to me, fresh, undiscov-
ered. It seemed beautiful and light, funny
and mysterious. It caught my attention
when nothing else could, not even chocolate. I was seeing love for the first time.
And I was seeing it in different ways, the
ways we miss it from moment to moment.
It would pass by me on the street, it was all
over me in the car when I'd cry on the way
home from exhaustion, it was next to me as
I spewed off more lies at the Door and
pecked away at my soul. It was behind me,
pushing me in front of the moment so that I
could see for myself that it was real. It was
in strangers that I had never met who said
things or noticed things about me I never
cared to think about.

For the first time in a long time the gig felt tough, harder than the
others. The nights moved slowly. The Door conversation bored
me. It was getting old, and I was getting tired of all the shit. I was
starting to feel. Just plain old feel. I started looking people in the
eye at the Door. I'd let people in I shouldn't have, people with a
heart, people with the wrong clothes on, people who were the
wrong color. All the people who were considered wrong. I started
seeing people in the crowd as just ordinary folks, everyday joes. I
stopped separating them by gender, by race, by groups, by clothes,

by power, by talent, by connections, and I started to see people. All equal, all one, all the same. I tried smiling at them when I greeted them. I asked them questions about their night. But I was losing it. I was slipping away with every person I saw as an equal and every person I saw outside of a category. The Door ain't about being equal. The Door isn't about being just or right. It's about judging people for who you think they ought to be. It's about finding a place to put them, choosing between anything that would separate them from the rest. If that meant the color of their skin or how much money they were worth or what job they had or how beautiful they were, then that meant they had a reason to enter. There was no room for guilt, and I was feeling guilty. I was on my way out. I couldn't see the lie anymore, and more importantly, I couldn't believe it.

The large brick building on the corner of Gower and Hollywood Boulevard was a place I never thought I'd end up. It had nothing to offer me except fear. Strange people were probably inside, so I thought, and I was much too dirty to even think of going inside. However, the power of the building itself was enough to make me wonder. I passed by this structure on a daily basis, wondering what the inside could hold for me. Would it forgive me, guide me somewhere new, because if that was the case, I wasn't sure if I wanted to change or even if I could possibly conceive the idea of forgiveness. It seemed like such a long journey to a faraway place. I knew my way around this earth, and I had spent most of my life being a survivor, so I prided myself on that. It seemed there were many of us, in and under this heading, and especially at night.

So, then, why the building? The building with the cross on top. The building with the stained-glass windows. The strong, powerful building. Because I wasn't surviving anymore. Because when it comes to the end, it's what you're willing to believe in that will save you. If you are truly a survivor, you believe in nothing but yourself. I wasn't sure if I was ready to give up my survivor title yet. I'd earned it. I'd gotten raped for it, I'd lied for it, I'd hurt people for it, I'd used people for it, and I'd lived for it until my soul and my heart had hardened. I wasn't going to give it up for some belief that someone else was going to take care of business. That's why the building was fearful, because there were people of faith inside. People who turned their lives over on a daily basis to someone else or something else. True survivors never turn their lives over to something or someone else. Because they just survive. They don't live. Living is what I thought all the other people did, all the other people that weren't me. But I wanted to live too, I wanted to wake up and have a positive thought instead of the usual overanalytical self that always got in the way. Yes, living, that's what I wanted. To live, just once, to let go, to not always just be barely hanging on by a thread. I didn't want to see that towering wall in front of me every moment of the day with every new plan to escape my hellish life. I wanted to look ahead and not always behind me. I wanted to take a breath and not have it depend on me; I wanted to be fed, I didn't want to eat. I wanted to be able to climb that wall in front of me instead of having it always around me, enclosing me with no hope and no way out. I wanted the voices of doubt to stop dancing in my head and tearing down my ideas to escape my past and turn away from the evil and darkness I had become so attracted to. But I needed to know how to live, and where to go to live, and how to find this living salvation that was supposedly inside of me, and anyway, I wasn't sure it was worth all that trouble searching for something that I had never experienced or witnessed before. I always thought it probably just looked like it was nice to live that way, like being on the other side of the fence for once and feeling like some American cereal ad on television, all happy and satisfied. But then I'd wake up from my dreams and see the gun on my night table and wonder if what was inside that building could really save me or was it just like the commercial, just a sixty-second spot in my brain.

V.O. NARRATOR
I had received a phone call from Charlotte
(the Jesus freak) that day asking if I would
join her at Hollywood Presbyterian Church
for a special service they were having. I had
not heard from Charlotte in months, and
the last thing on my mind was church. I
thought I would return her call and tell her
I was sorry that I could not make it. I
dialed her number, expecting her machine,
when Charlotte answered. The sound of her
sweet voice answering the phone prompted
me to accept her invitation reluctantly.
There was no getting out of it. I had let
Charlotte down so many times I knew this
would be the last time she would be calling.
I felt relieved and scared all at the same
time that I would have to face Charlotte
and church together. Was I ready to come
clean, I thought to myself, was I ready to
tell the truth and not always lie? Was I
ready at all, I wondered, for any of it?

I had my black leather jacket on, the kind my father used to wear in the sixties when he'd pick me up for the weekends in his black Cadillac with the red interior; he called it a car coat. I wore my black leather motorcycle boots, jeans, dark glasses and blonde hair. That's how I walked down the aisle. I sat back four rows from the altar with Charlotte. I waited in silence for church to start. I was tired, broken, and hopeless.

The choir entered row by row, wearing robes and carrying hymn books. I held the program tightly in my hand, not knowing what to do with it. Then the music started, a soft, beautiful hymn that grew in size and volume until finally tapering off to a silent finish. I didn't understand what they were singing about, I just felt the music. It spoke softly, then powerfully, then quietly, then it came to a dead stop. It was the music of my life, and for those very few minutes I felt something different in myself, I felt my heart beating and my legs weaken as my head dropped to my chest to ask for forgiveness. I heard nothing but silence as I lifted my eyes to the ceiling out of my shame and unholy state, hoping that God would see me there all alone and maybe meet me halfway. The pews were hard, my shoulders hurt, my hair still smelled of smoke, and my pockets were filled with the shame and reminders of who I was and who I had become. "Let us pray."

I had stalkers for years, and some who followed me from club to club. But it was always the same old drill; I knew who they were and there were always the guys to protect me. I always had my walkie-talkie, my gun, my bulletproof vest, I had training, I knew how to defend myself if I was attacked at the Door, and I also had a very big ego that I was sure could protect me. So I had no worries about the recent pulls from the Door. They were routine, a few days off, then back to normal until the next death threat, then a few days off again, and then it would be over for a couple months before they'd start up again.

But all of my serious death threats came in the form of phone calls during the day, warning the club that something terrible would happen to me if I were at the Door that night, and that's all it would take for them to pull me. But Saturday afternoon I didn't get the call from the club not to come in, things had been going okay for a few weeks and I wasn't worried. But as I dressed for Saturday night, the call came in, there had been a death threat, and it was from the same stalker who had been calling all the previous weeks. The club was fed up with it, however; he was costing them money to pull me from the Door and they were sure that nothing was going to happen. So as I was driving my car to work and setting up the ropes, my stalker was filling a beer bottle with sand and staking out a place in which to hide until that one second in which I'd be alone for him. Security had not been informed of any threats. As far as we knew, it was just another Saturday night.

It was mid-November, the week before Thanksgiving. It was cold in Los Angeles and we were freezing at the Door. The wind was blowing chills through our bodies. We all had dressed as warm as we could, but it wasn't fending off the late night dampness from the coastal breezes that filled the after-hours air. I had three guys with me outside and a whole crew inside. Every twenty minutes I would let one of the guys go in to get a coffee or use the rest room. They rotated themselves while I ran the Door. It was a slow night for a Saturday. It was too cold for Angelenos to come out. By one o'clock the line had cleared. There was no one waiting. We always had a rule at the front that I would never be without two guys. But I made the rules, so therefore I could change them. And the colder it got, the easier it became. I sent two guys inside for coffee and a shot of tequila for me. That left me and one security man. We shot the shit as we waited. We got ETAs on the coffee and tequila on line two and listened as security bullshitted about the blonde with the tit that had burst last Friday night on the dance floor. Inside they had begun shutting down the upstairs bar, and the DJ was playing loud closing music to push the crowds home.

That's when I heard the call. "Dance floor, main bar, left side." Black Eye, a retired burned-out police officer, had always taken the dance floor as his post, and he was calling for help on line one. Generally, if there was a problem, Inside could see it, find it and handle it. Tonight, Inside didn't see or hear the call. The fight was growing in size and getting violent. Beer bottles were being thrown at the fight from upstairs, tables and chairs were being overturned, girls were running and screaming toward the exits, and still no help had arrived. Black Eye's continued cry for help on line one had gone unanswered. I had to make a decision. Send Black Eye into the fight and leave the dance floor unprotected with hundreds of people screaming in panic as the crowd grew more and more aware of the fight, or send my last security man at the Front Door toward the fight and leave myself alone at the Door. I chose to be left alone. If ever I was left at the Door alone, I was to go inside and lock the Door. I did not. I stood and I waited for security to return, and I called the police.

V.O. NARRATOR

I didn't see him come out from anywhere, I
didn't hear anything, I just turned around
and he was right there in front of me. I
reached for my walkie-talkie and he
reached for my neck. I reached back up to
grab his wrists and break them away from
the choke hold that he had on me, but I
tripped backward and went through the
glass doors with him on top of me, still
holding my neck. He released his grip from
my neck as we fell to the ground on the
shattered glass, and he put his hand into
his overcoat and pulled a green beer bottle
filled with sand headed toward my face,
and as he lifted his arm over his head with

the beer bottle, that's when I felt it again, I felt something move my head to the left, and the bottle came down toward my face and missed. And then the feeling was gone as fast as it came. The next thing I remember were fifteen security men beating the shit out of my stalker and hearing the sirens on the police cars coming closer. I got up on my own, I wouldn't accept a hand from security. I noticed my list on the floor by the Door with glass shattered all over it, I pulled my walkie-talkie out of my coat pocket and set it on the bar, I ripped my vest off, I unstrapped my shoulder strap and laid the gun next to it. I didn't answer any questions, I just saw mouths moving at me and in front of me. I noticed my cut hands, and I felt something wrong with my leg. I don't think I was breathing yet, I think I was just waiting to breathe like a child that waits in the womb to be born. I signed some paper the police put in front of me and watched them handcuff my stalker, now bloody from the beating. Still I remained quiet and did not speak. The guys spoke for me, to me, about me, and around me. The owners spoke with the police, the staff returned to cleaning up and shutting down the club, the music was silenced, the last customers were hurried out the back Door, and still, while all this went on, I remained frozen at the bar, staring at the Door which I had just gone through. The Door that had changed my whole life forever was now gone, shattered. And I was the one who'd broken it. I don't think it was really the stalker who pushed me through that Door, even though in this life it looks that way, but I'm glad it broke, 'cause it broke me, too. It broke the bond I had with it, and it broke the ego I had that kept it going for so long. I didn't say good night to the guys, I didn't say good-bye to the owners, I just walked through the broken glass and out my last Door. I kept walking until I hit the edge of the beach. As I came closer to the ocean and felt the sand under my feet, I peeled off each layer of clothing on the way down to the ocean. Layers of shame, layers of guilt, layers of regret, and all the layers that kept me weighed down for years. When I reached the ocean's edge with only my T-shirt and boots on, I begged for forgiveness. I had survived and I had learned to be a survivor from all of my experiences. However, I had never learned to live and forgive myself for all I had done and all others had done to me. I had to choose in that moment when I was going through that glass Door to live or die, and I chose to live, to love, to forgive, to laugh, to cry, and to wonder how someone like me got so lucky to live such a great and interesting fucked-up life . . . and you know what I think? I don't think it was luck at all. I chose to open that Door night after night, just like all the Doors we open and shut in our lives that make up one life. I know now. You can open many Doors in your life, but it's the ones that you shut that will make the difference.

Like this is the only one...

Floating
Robin Troy

The Fuck-up
Arthur Nersesian

Dreamworld
Jane Goldman

Fake Liar Cheat
Tod Goldberg

Dogrun
Arthur Nersesian

Brave New Girl
Louisa Luna

The Foreigner
Meg Castaldo

Tunnel Vision
Keith Lowe

Number Six Fumbles
Rachel Solar-Tuttle

Crooked
Louisa Luna

Don't Sleep with Your Drummer
Jen Sincero

Thin Skin
Emma Forrest

Last Wave
Paul Hayden

More from the young, the hip,
and the up-and-coming.
Brought to you by MTV Books.

POCKET
BOOKS

© 2003 MTVN

The Alphabetical Hookup List

A new series

A–J
K–Q
R–Z

Three sizzling titles
Available from
PHOEBE McPHEE
and MTV Books

www.mtv.com
www.alloy.com

As many as one in three
Americans with HIV...
DO NOT KNOW IT.

More than half of those
who will get HIV this year...
ARE UNDER 25.

HIV is preventable.
You can help fight AIDS.
Get informed. Get the facts.

www.knowhivaids.org
1-866-344-KNOW